Crisis to Riches

JOHN RANIOLA

ISBN: 9798559496702 (paperback)

Imprint: Independently published
Author John Raniola
All rights reserved Self-Heal and Become Success Corp.

One day you wake up with a vision in a money world telling you that to change the world "the good people" need to possess money—and lots of it—which inspired me to a new level of meaningful purpose that directed me to write this text.

Contents

Acknowledgments		vii
About John Raniola		ix
1	Belief	1
2	Secrets	17
3	Purpose vs. Meaningful Purpose	24
4	Crisis to Riches	29
5	Strength of Forgiveness	34
6	Definitions	36
7	Transforming Reality	43
8	Message	49
9	Law of Accepting	56
10	Lonely Road to Success	60
11	The Spiraling Effect	63
12	Guide of Divine	71
13	Master Mind	84
14	Vision	95
15	Self-Discipline	104
16	Institutionalized	113
17	The Hidden Truth	118
18	Final Chapter	123

Acknowledgments

I want to thank the Napoleon Hill Foundation for keeping one of the world's most excellent success philosophies alive today, which helped transform my entire life (Naphill.org).

I want to thank all the Napoleon Hill brothers and sisters of the PMA Science of Success philosophy.

"I went to the Napoleon Hill Foundation, looking for knowledge, and came home with a family."

I want to thank Don Green of the Napoleon Hill Foundation for being a beacon of light to me and others. Don has released what I believe is one of the most influential books by Napoleon Hill—*Outwitting the Devil*. Don Green's passion and work with the Napoleon Hill Foundation guided me.

I want to thank Rosetta Q from Think and Grow Rich, Caribbean, and Jamaica. I want to thank Hugo De La Torre at Think and Grow Rich, Columbia.

I want to thank my Global Team colleagues: Sandra Valencia, Lefford Fate, Amanda Forslund, Alejandra Miranda, Johnnie Lioyd, and Kimberly Coots.

I would like to thank my Napoleon Hill sister that gave me a tremendous opportunity to speak across the globe, Amanda Forslund, at Think and Grow Rich Sweden. This experience contributed to my wisdom and success.

Amanda, your strength, fantastic attitude, and energy inspired many and genuinely inspired me. May you rest in peace, and may you guide us all from the spiritual world.

I want to thank anyone writing or talking about self-development and healing on social media. I have taken in so much information that has helped me to evolve into the person I am today. I also want to thank my spiritual guides and messengers for life's success.

Most importantly, I want to thank you, the reader, and my success philosophy followers.

About John Raniola

I am a transformational author, business owner, speaker, coach, certified Reiki master and certified Napoleon Hill Science of Success instructor and leader.

I found myself lost in life, living out my dad's definition of success. I had it all—the secure union job, pension, 401k, investments, the house, new cars, endless overtime. I had it all; I created my dad's image of success.

But I found myself lost, becoming a workaholic and unable to face reality or my inner wounds; working hard was all I knew. I gave up my life and relationships with the job.

In 2013, I recognized I was missing something in my life, and I started my search. At first, my vision was to become super rich and show off my wealth.

During my journey, I began to work toward money and material objects, and I started to drill into my mind any self-help, get-rich finance books I could find. I listened to motivational speakers. I was determined to find the answers that I needed to better my life.

At the beginning of the year 2014, I finally built up the courage to quit my union job and set up my heating and air-conditioning company, Raniola Mechanical & Maintenance Corp.

During this journey of becoming a business owner, I learned a lot about myself and others. I recognized self-sabotage patterns, fears, limited beliefs, and negative habits. Most important of all, I found what controlled my reality.

I kept a messy journal of information from this remarkable transformation. That unorganized journal became the book *Self-Heal and Become Success*. Writing this book taught me a lot about myself.

The title of the book came to me at the end of the proofreading. At that time, I realized I was the only key to happiness, and it was me that was self-healing myself and my past and my ancestors' belief patterns. I was beginning to self-heal myself rich.

For the first time in my life, I found myself returning to my dreams, ideas, self, and I started to uncover my meaningful purpose.

My journey guided me toward becoming a business owner and getting certified as a Napoleon Hill Science of Success instructor and leader. I also found myself studying and becoming a certified Reiki master.

I put my lifetime of wisdom in guiding others toward self-healing their past patterns and redirecting their success toward a meaningful purpose. I have reached a new level, and this new level begins with this book.

I recently realized we go through levels toward growing our success, and I recognized I was more focused on healing my past than on redirecting my financial future. Yes, I was growing every day. Yes, I was changing the world. Still, someplace inside, I was held down by finances, limiting beliefs about money—imprinted in my sub-conscience mind for lifetimes—causing me to build debt. Almost sending me back to working for someone else.

I realized that the right people are not winning in a money world held back by limited belief systems. Money is power, money is good, and money is evil. Money can be healthy and can be harmful. Remember, we can be rich and live a destructive lifestyle.

Money can be a sword. God came to me in my dreams in a vision, and I felt God revealed to me that He wants me and other good people to be rich with money, and the concept for this book was born. It takes money to heal the cash world. We must stop fooling ourselves.

As a certified Napoleon Hill Foundation PMA (positive mental attitude) Science of Success certified leader and instructor, you will find some of Napoleon Hill's philosophy explained within my journey. I not only read Napoleon Hill's philosophy but also put his teaching into action, traveling toward and unveiling my meaningful purpose. I have also spent the last eight years learning and teaching myself while developing my life, lifestyle, mental and physical healing, creating money, and building businesses.

Many coaches sell you your excuses. A few will sell "you" to you and may shorten the time it takes to grow into your success. The people that are going to succeed will do so with a coach or not. The great will guide you to what you already know and will sell you confidence or, as I like to call it, a helping hand. Like all my writings and teachings, I can only be a helping hand that can guide you. It is up to you to build faith in yourself and your desires and direct your success with action. I have tried and studied many success tools, and I will explain many throughout this book. And these tools should guide you toward your ideas. I will also explain in depth many of these so-called "secret" success tools.

1

Belief

Thoughts and emotions pulled in all directions.

I started to put this book together during the coronavirus pandemic of 2020—a time of a lot of uncertainty.

I questioned myself. Inside of the pandemic of 2020. Why are many people creating new riches for themselves and their families while many others are falling apart? And how can I help guide others toward a direction of transformation in today's world?

A mind divided by itself cannot succeed.

With all that is going on in this pandemic, everybody is giving instructions: do this, don't do that. Many professionals are giving advice. Life coaches advise do this, don't do this. My religion is better than yours. Politicians are fighting back and forth. This limited belief over this limited belief. No wonder why we are confused about making money and how to create our dreams. Our minds are too busy focusing on the nonsense and labels, aka BS.

To develop riches, one needs to focus primarily on

making money within the law of accepting money; some will call this a secret; some will call this the law of success or the law of attraction or manifesting. Some may even call it God or the Universe. I call it the Guide of Divine.

What dominates our focus, we become.

It is time to cut out all the crap that you do not need in your life and direct yourself toward the money you want and deserve. Yes, you may have been told not to focus on the money. I will also call this BS. Believe me when I tell you my journey put me through many different levels. First, I wanted a lot of money; second, I tried to heal the world as an excuse. But I was not ready to heal myself. Third, I healed myself; fourth, I turned my focus on money. Why? Unless you are a saint, you will need money to improve the world and yourself. Yes, my friends, money wealth is what makes this money world go around. Stop pretending it doesn't.

We all have belief systems that were repeatedly delivered to us from our past generations and societies and present communities. Let us not forget about the media. Everyone is in the fight for your sale, and, sadly, many choose to buy the negative.

I know what you are saying. Maybe the fastest way to becoming wealthy is to sell the negative? Later on, in this book, I hope to show you why I do not believe this is a great idea. Besides, when you take from those that are not ready, something will be taken from you. It is true that if you give, it is given back to you in some form. It is also true that when you take something, something is taken from you in some way.

Limiting beliefs are chaining our dreams away.

We tend to beg God to do things we are not willing or too lazy to do ourselves. We beg for miracles. We pray for comfortable lives; we beg for cash; we beg for health. We also wonder why things happen when they happen and wonder why that person never received a miracle. It is the same thing as not having training in the art of recognizing opportunities.

Miracles, manifesting, and opportunities are all one. They are available to those that have been trained to see the hidden truth in front of their eyes, and if you cannot see them in front of you, the mind's eye can teach you how to recognize opportunities through all of your senses.

No, I am not talking about the third eye. One needs to understand the entire body's nerve system and mind points. Thoughts and emotions become a reality through these systems. I am not a doctor; I believe it to be common sense once one understands the hidden truth.

Maybe that failure was an opportunity, a miracle, and we became blind or addicted to giving up; then we beg for strength again and fail again or give up over and over. We became starters but feared finishing or feared success. Many live a life with the habit of giving up (failing). For some, it is easier to fall than it is to rise or face their dreams. Dreams scare many into living a mediocre life.

We live a life of harmful practices, and maybe we received

a miracle after a miracle only to find out the benefits eventually run out. We need to learn how to see gifts and opportunities. Every moment opportunities and information are right in front of us. We are receiving that miracle that we strive for, but maybe we are shutting down or ignoring the messenger.

Miracles and messengers hide within the level of our lifestyle, and our lifestyle will radiate a new level of blessings or opportunities. Aka law of attraction.

Limited beliefs very well can be destructive. What if I told you different levels of limited ideas exist and that they have created reality while running on autopilot? This chapter will open your mind toward understanding how easy it is for even the smallest limited belief, saying, or quote to affect your entire world. Throughout this book, the tools revealed can reverse these belief systems and help you to make more money and achieve a blissful state of mind.

Money is evil.

How many of us have heard money is the root of all evil from someone that was not rich? Cash is only evil if the mind that is controlling it is harmful to itself or others. The mindset is mostly governed by money.

Not having money or living in poverty has made many people evil. Some people are just evil, and some people are sinners.

Money only amplifies attitudes and lifestyles.

The level of the mindset and your definition of morals is a reflection of your money.

If you accept that money is evil and you want to grow rich, why would you ever accept riches into your life? Think about that. Money is great. Let us shift one limited belief right now. Money is the root of all good. Money is good.

Money is spent energy and time in storage.

It takes time and energy to build your finances. The longer you hold yourself back because of limiting beliefs that have filled your thoughts throughout your day and nights over a lifetime and possible for generations, the more is the time wasted.

We only get one life. And we are all rich in time—negative time, or the right time. We are wealthy with what we spend our time on. Look around, and you will see many are rich in poverty and illnesses and have a harmful lifestyle. And I will bet they live by it.

It is up to you to shift your situations and beliefs. No one is going to do it for you.

A stale and idle mind keeps you in the same world and may even push you backward. We can spiral our way toward prosperity or spiral our way toward a poisonous mental and physical death. If we are not growing, we are fading away.

Time is money, and boy, do we have the habit of throwing or giving away our time on social media, news, TV, the Internet, negative people that we can never change, and yes, the newly found healers that have drained their own time and energy on those that will never help themselves. It is a human trait to get excited when we learn something new, especially when we learn how to release/transform heavy energy, thought, and emotional patterns. The first thing we seem to do is become an excited kid that received a gift and goes out and plays the "show and tell" game.

Learn about your energy and others' energy; learn who drains you and who makes you grow. Remember, you can help only those that are willing to help themselves. I have watched people give and give to takers. Takers are the people that will never share back; they take and take. For many of those drained, I have found they have been needy of giving deep within. It filled a void like a drug. We will discuss this later in the book in the chapter of the law of accepting. Later, you will also understand why I tell my readers and students to ignore the law of attraction.

Time and energy are essential because you need to use them to create a plan and work on yourself and your dreams. It is fantastic when your mind goes into saving mode and you start looking for more valuable time; the time wasted starts to fade away, and more time is spent on being productive.

If every day cannot be a productive day, at least have more productive days than unproductive days. In time you will find the law of motion will start to take over, and soon your weaker days will fade away.

When you realize how expensive your time is and that you only have so much time left to create your dreams and why this book is about manifesting/building a financial mindset, it is time for a shift to occur in this world. Because it is a money world, funds are essential.

Your time can be worth billions if you spend your time toward creating billions.

Take the limited belief that money is not needed to make you happy; yes, correct. One can become satisfied alone in a padded room if, in their mind, one is glad and delighted with the life in a padded room. Unless you win the lottery or look for handouts, you will need to create cash to live in this money world.

If you are like me and have ideas to be delivered out of your mind and into reality, you will have to work hard and establish a team that you will have to pay toward creating whatever your desires are.

For example, this book did not come from magic; I used up time, money, energy, and some of my life to create this book. I had to have the money to hire the editors and printers and put in advertisements etc. without knowing if rewards other than self-wisdom would enter my life from this text.

All I can tell you is I am growing and bettering myself every moment of my life. Call me greedy, but I want my time to be spent in building a smarter, higher, and more successful me. I wasted enough of my life on the negative, harmful lifestyle and spent money on useless nights and objects I used only once—life, time, and energy that I will never get back. Exactly why three years ago, I said I would never have another sip of alcohol. I like who I am becoming, and I do not want to miss one-thousandth of a second from my new reality.

Limiting beliefs can be small and can be destructive.

We are now beginning to learn how to control some

of these minor beliefs, sayings, stories, which have held down generations, countries, and perhaps most of the world. Now we know we can start shifting the ideas that will eventually turn our realities and the realities all around us. Remember, the shift will have a rippling effect for the future, the same rippling effect from our past wherein limited beliefs chained us and our ancestors down from true desires.

We are starting to see how the words we speak create our worlds and that we can talk ourselves rich if we only begin to believe and develop or grow our practices successfully.

Let us play a game. List some simple beliefs that hold down others, or even yourself. After you get a few big ones down on paper, dig deeper and study the words people speak and how they live in their reality. You should begin to see the patterns being repeated right in front of your eyes. It would help if you realized there are only a few patterns in the world—repeated repeatedly by the masses.

Also, you should begin to recognize if they are spiraling out of control in autopilot or spiraling in control, and you may even find a few succeeding in a blissful autopilot mode. It is up to you to control your patterns and redirect those patterns toward your desires or bettering yourself.

Past down from parents to children

Sometimes we put sayings into the minds of our children, and we do not know where these sayings came from—maybe something someone else said. "Never depend on a man." If the mind of a young lady hears this enough number of times, she will start believing it. You may learn that this alone may hold women down from revealing the level of the hidden truths of real success to live the lives they have been born into. Yes, maybe they will be phenomenally successful in a career or business and find that one day they traded their family desires away, so they never depended on a man.

For the man, my dad's saying was "Be a man." Many men have learned to suppress their emotions. Maybe the imprinted belief was men do not cry, men are tough, never trust anyone, etc. these belief systems most likely have destroyed many dreams and relationships.

When we lose our internal plans, we lose a part of ourselves.

Maybe limiting beliefs can cause anxiety, stress, and worry, allowing one's hidden drive for real success to fade away. Perhaps some will become medicated and become very content with the world given to them by others. I am not a doctor; only what I believe would have happened if I had turned to medication instead of pushing toward a meaningful purpose, shifting my life definition, or how I let my mind define my reality.

The most anxiety and panic attacks I have ever had was while sitting in two to six hours a day in bumper-to-bumper traffic, and I felt I was eating my life away. I thought I was supposed to be so much more. I always asked myself what went wrong.

Another part of my anxiety was that I did the math, and the math told me that from that day to retirement, I would spend four years of my life sitting in traffic. And I was very generous with the travel time. The truth is four years would have probably been the minimum of my life spent in traffic.

At that time, my life was about a paycheck, for my dad always told me work was necessary. He would also talk me out of going to family funerals because it would have interfered with work. To my dad, working and the job always came first. A belief passed on to me.

This attitude did not go well when I was dating and turned down their family's funerals or family functions for work. Belief is powerful, especially when it comes from people you look up to; and it can be destructive, especially in relationships.

Women. The only experience I have is through dating. Those ladies did end up putting all their efforts into a career, some at the cost of never having babies and families.

Can you see the foolishness and how limited beliefs destroy dreams? Most beliefs, if not all, have been passed to us by the previous generation. Why again, I will tell you to ignore the attraction in the law of attraction.

When I was speaking at the Think and Grow Rich Sweden, one of the students talked about a law that held down the people of the surrounding countries. Now me being from America, I asked if this was a government law. This person and the class laughed and said no, it was not a government law. "So," I asked in surprise, "why would you let a fake law hold you down?" The answer I received was "fear of criticism." This moment was when I realized how powerful a limited belief system could be. It was the moment when

I grew into a new level of meaningful purpose to destroy limited beliefs globally.

It did not matter if it were false or accurate, or a story that could keep someone from all of their potentials. This law is called the Law Jante.

The Law of Jante.
From Wikipedia, the free encyclopedia.
https://en.wikipedia.org/wiki/Law_of_Jante
Jump to navigationJump to search
*The **Law of Jante** (Danish: Janteloven)[note 1] is a literary element that has been assumed by some to explain the egalitarian nature of Nordic countries.[1] It characterizes not conforming, doing things out of the ordinary, or being personally ambitious as unworthy and inappropriate. The attitudes were first formulated in the form of the ten rules of Jante Law by the Dano-Norwegian author Aksel Sandemose in his satirical novel* A Fugitive Crosses His Tracks (En flyktning krysser sitt spor, *1933), but the actual attitudes themselves are older.[2] Sandemose portrays the fictional small Danish town of Jante, which he modeled upon his native town Nykøbing Mors in the 1930s, where nobody was anonymous, a feature of life typical of all small towns and communities.[3]*

Used generally in colloquial speech in the Nordic countries as a sociological term to denote a social attitude of disapproval toward expressions of individuality and personal Success, it emphasizes adherence to the collective.[4]

The ten rules state:

1. *You're not to think you are anything special.*
2. *You're not to think you are as good as we are.*
3. *You're not to think you are smarter than we are.*
4. *You're not to imagine yourself better than we are.*
5. *You're not to think you know more than we do.*
6. *You're not to think you are more important than we are.*
7. *You're not to think you are good at anything.*
8. *You're not to laugh at us.*
9. *You're not to think anyone cares about you.*
10. *You're not to think you can teach us anything.*

The Janters who transgress this unwritten "law" are regarded with suspicion and some hostility, as it goes against the town's communal desire to preserve harmony, social stability, and uniformity.

An eleventh rule recognized in the novel as "the penal code of Jante" is:

11. *Perhaps you don't think we know a few things about you?*

From the chapter "Maybe you don't think I know something about you":

That one sentence (the eleventh rule), which acts as the penal code of Jante, as such was rich in content. It was a charge of all sorts of things, and that it also had to be, because absolutely nothing was allowed. It was also an elaborate *indictment, with all kinds of unspecified penalties given to be expected. Furthermore it was useful, depending fully on tone of voice, in financial extortion and enticement into criminal acts, and it could also be the best means of defense.*

♦ ♦ ♦

In the beginning, was the word, and the word was with God, and the word was God.
—John 1:1-14

We can see how a book, someone's words wrong or right, can hold down generations and even countries, maybe even the entire world. Every definition we hear and the stories that we speak can become us. The "word" is powerful and can be destructive, and words can travel forever through the human generations, shaping the world. At the beginning of creating is the "word," and its definition grows real. The word is the seed. The description is what grows. The beginning of belief. The beginning of manifesting and creation.

Those who control the definitions of the words rule the world.

The so-called secret tools to success are also tools toward the negative. Be very careful who and what you allow to feed your mind. If you are not in control, someone or something else is.

Can fear be a limited belief system that can control many? What feeds fear, and how do we reverse fearing something into something that we can use to thrive? If we genuinely want to succeed, we need to remove everything that we cannot change from our focus and learn how to direct and fill our minds with the visions of our desires and things we can control.

Some people love fear and hate and are addicted to it, and if repeated enough number of times. Fear and hate can define you.

People need excuses for not succeeding, and if you are not careful, people will sell you those excuses, which is why you must turn off the news. Similarly, if everything you see from anyone on social media is negative, run from it because it just may become you. Remember the Law of Jante which was repeated through countries and generations until it got imprinted in the minds of many. If I am wrong about the media and the media was positive, I ask what percentage are happy stories?

On top of that, every other commercial mentioned is a disease and a bunch of side effects. I do not think I need to explain how words create realities. Especially for those lost and in need of a purpose. I have watched people argue about who is the winner in having the most ailments. There is such a thing as negative affirmation.

What if the media is a form of the vision board for the negative seeking a purpose? Yes, many live out harmful life purposes. There is a significant difference in seeking others' intentions and building yourself into a meaningful purpose.

Level of fear. I want to make this very clear: if you watch the media or watch any salesman, you will find they are looking to take something from you and not supply what you genuinely need or they try to sell you a program they know you will never use or will wipe out your bank account or add credit to your credit cards. You may find there is division, fear, or hate.

Fear and separation sell. I would do some research on the fight-or-flight syndrome. As a businessperson, when I sell, I sell the customer what is needed. As if I were a friend. I have very excellent customers. Watch out for sales tactics. Some motivational teachers are more of a salesperson than a teacher.

We can face foolish fears, freeze ourselves in ice water, jump out of a plane, or walk on fire. However, overcoming these fears may not help you overcome the obstacles in the path of your success.

I have trained in martial arts. I would step into the ring and spar. Even in the street, I did not fear any man. I was angry at the world. I spent enough of my life being pushed around as a child. I remember a saying on the martial arts dojos wall that repeated in my mind repeatedly; that quote became an affirmation for training and life: "I come with empty hands, and I fear no man."

At that time, it was easier for me to go into a fight-to-my-death mode than ask the women I dreamed about for a date. I never dared to quit my job. Sometimes we may need to bring down some of our beliefs a level or two. What I am saying is, go after real fears, the fears that hold you from your dreams.

All the world's motivation is worthless if you never take the initiative to turn that motivation into action toward what you desire.

Exercise:

Let us take a few limited beliefs we need to transform and write the opposite of that belief positively. For example, "Keeping up with the Jones" causes many to overspend and put stress on one's families and lives. One way of changing the focus from others to yourself is to affirm, "The only one I compete with is myself. Every moment I create a better version of myself in all that I am and all I do."

Limited Beliefs	Positive Beliefs

2

Secrets

Almost every place I look and everything I read; someone is talking about some secret to riches. Throughout this book, you will find how to find these so-called hidden riches that millions are searching for and have tried to find. It has caused many to give up their dreams and has directed many to financial wealth. Let the journey begin. We are about to unravel the hidden mysteries to reveal all the mysteries of success. First, I would like to tell you that it took me years of searching to discover the truth about winning and understand the mysteries of manifesting and attracting. Get ready, because I will reveal years of thousands upon thousands of dollars and trial and error that led me to understand the hocus-pocus of success. Get ready. Abracadabra.

Chasing secrets to success is a fool's journey.

What do I mean when I say chasing a secret is a fool's journey? I used to seek some secret or search for someone to do the work for me throughout my journey. This resulted in a lot of effort to get rich—selling people programs that people would most likely never complete and search for another.

Many people read self-development books repeatedly and buy new ones without ever doing the texts' exercises.

Did the journey of chasing a hidden mystery help me create confidence in myself? Yes, it did, but, at the same time, it trapped me and held me down from my dreams. The mind is a powerful place and wants to play with us.

You ask what the secret to success is, and people give you different answers trying to explain something that cannot be explained in words, for real success needs to be described within the experience.

Remove all definitions. What is natural law? Growth, even destruction, is a growing process. We can shift every crisis into an asset if we learn how to control and shift our thinking. Even in death we can turn an end into a blessing.

Napoleon Hill wrote the book *Think and Grow Rich*. Our minds focus on the "think and rich" part and skip the "grow" part in the title. To grow is the answer you seek. One must grow in knowledge, wisdom, actions, courage, etc. The one thing I have found is that as I grew forward, I started to heal my past patterns which in turn began to transform my future. I felt I needed to call my first book, *Self-Heal and Become Success*.

It is our past patterns that have created our reality and will build our future in some form, if we never learn how to control our patterns, emotions, thoughts, beliefs, and other things that direct us when we do not witness our lives or, one may say, run on autopilot.

The question you must be asking now is, how can I run my success on autopilot?

To understand more about what it takes to grow rich,

one must understand a little bit about how the mind works. First, I am not a doctor, and I doubt anyone knows 100 percent of what the mind is or how it works. Many have tried to explain it and have confused many. I hope to explain it from my perspective through my experience and the tools given in this book. Keep in mind I may be wrong. I am still growing and self-healing my past. All I ask is to keep your mind open, think for yourself, and always level up the knowledge you receive through experiences.

An open mind opens other minds. A closed mind slams other minds closed.

When you have an open mind, others will open their minds to you; close your mind or look for an argument, and you slam successful minds shut, especially if successful people have no time for arguments or games. They have found how much their time is worth.

If you believe there is a secret to success that only the rich know, you may always seek a mystery.

The mind wants to believe that a hidden mystery to making money is real—some mystic potion, some magical way to be rich. Our minds want to play games with us. Our brain is like a child and does not know the difference between negative or positive, riches or poverty; it wants to give us what we tell it over and over. Yes, it also wants to provide us with what others have told us over and over that we allowed our minds to believe.

One can be rich without money, but if one has not been born in cash, one must become wealthy with money. One cannot just be money rich. To become is to grow into someone.

> *What the mind can conceive and believe the mind can achieve.*
> —Napoleon Hill

It is a funny thing. It is said never tell anyone what the secret is. I believe this to be an inside joke. Sadly, one cannot recognize the secret until one is prepared to understand the secret/mystery/unknown. Almost every book, including my first book, says this, and right after, it gives you the secret in some definition. For me, it took years for my mind to register it, even when it was right in front of my eyes.

What is it your mind is conceiving at this moment?
Are you starting to find what you believed in before you started this book has changed somewhat already? If so, you have just shifted your thinking and changed how you witnessed something that caused you to shift your belief slightly, and if you add action toward growing this new adjusted belief, what can you accomplish? Napoleon Hill's quote says, "can achieve"; it does not say "will achieve."

Read Napoleon Hill's quote again and again. And if you are reading Napoleon Hill's work, highlight this quote in the book.

I believe that believing in a secret to happiness cost me thousands upon thousands of dollars and years of my life searching for a mystery that should reveal itself to you throughout these texts. What I can tell you is that I believe this book is going to be a shortcut. I hope it will cut out years of foolish games. But the games may be what I needed to find the confidence in myself. It may be what inspired me to keep going in the beginning.

What I can tell you is that my mind believed in a secret, and my mind wanted to give me what I felt. So, the game for the secrets began, and my journey toward success started. The transformation had begun. I will tell you even though the mind played the games, the mind, whatever it is, did eventually teach me how to develop and understand the secret to happiness and to build wealth. I found the hidden truth in my journey of growing and self-healing my past. At least I found myself witnessing that my past was controlling my actions.

I was tricked into self-healing and transforming my mindset, lifestyle, and belief systems. And most importantly, it taught me how to redirect the patterns of beliefs, emotions, traumas, and everything else delivered to me by my past generations and social surroundings.

Those that built the past delivered their creation toward our generation. Who we are today, we package it toward our next generations, for we became creators.

If you can understand the above quote, you can understand more about the hidden truth and redirect your mindset and beliefs toward more money and happiness. As I wrote above, the life puzzle will reveal itself when you are prepared to understand it. The hidden truth is growth, and it will take work in the mind and action in reality.

We live in two worlds, one in the mind and one in existence. The only thing you need to do is learn how to take control of both worlds.

The secret to success is to trick someone into success. I am starting to believe the saying, "Never reveal the secrets to getting rich." Is it the secret to success.

It is better that you believe a secret to success exists because if you understood what it took for me to dig myself out of the old me, your dreams would probably scare you to being "normal."

Foolish people like to play games. Truth is, it is not foolish people, but only untrained minds that look for the easy way of life or believe freedom in life is supposed to be handed to them. The trained mind plays the game of life, "success." Choose your game wisely.

For one to accept and respect real financial success, one must earn it.

The only way to achieve total freedom is through the development of the mind. A closed mind cannot see. A mind that allows others to do its thinking for them is blind. To grow your financial and life success, one must open the mind. One must train the mind to see into the unknown. The unknown is the place where the hidden truth hides. The only difference between the unsuccessful and the successful ones is what the mind sees.

We need to see our world as different worlds or different levels. The people on the lower levels cannot see what you see on the level you are on, and you cannot see what the people see on the floors above you. If you can understand this, you can understand the mind. The question one must ask is, how do I level up when I cannot see it yet?

They say you become the five books you read and the five people you surround yourself with. But this does not tell you how to get yourself there. I would love to hang out with Warren Buffet, Bill Gates, Donald Trump, Elon Musk, and Jeff Bezos. Imagine tapping into these minds together. However, I doubt I will meet anyone on the list above anytime soon. If I am lucky enough, let me rephrase that I will probably encounter one or two of them in person if I am successful enough. At this time I will have to settle with books and my vision of my success.

Throughout this book, you will find the tools used by the most successful people in America. You will find that the founders of America secretly implanted the hidden truth to America's success for those ready to recognize and grow into a higher understanding. Many Americans have risen to new levels, revealing the hidden blueprints of America.

The secret to freedom is hidden in plain sight and can be easily seen, which is why one must watch out for people that demonize others. The mind wants to play games with you; the mind is youthful and has no clue about the difference between the negative and the positive or growth and destruction, and the only way to change anything is to change the direction of how your mind grows. Remember, thoughts and emotions can destroy one if that is the direction one chooses to travel.

If it is not an asset, throw it out.

3

Purpose vs. Meaningful Purpose

If you do not have a purpose, be careful because someone will give you one.

We all have a purpose. Only a few will live out a meaningful purpose.

What if I told you if not today but, one day, you may be able to see that some people are in a self-destructive/self-sabotage/negative lifestyle purpose and believe it is normal? Some may even think they are successful. It could be you at this time.

My definition of meaningful purpose is growing into the person I have been born to become and having the means to hire those willing to help me build my dreams into reality. With that, I can change or heal the world.

We have this limited belief that money is evil. If we demonize the rich, why would we be guided to money riches? Better yet, if we believe money will make us happier, we may spend all our life searching for more cash rather than looking for happiness—because our definition of happiness is money or material objects.

Money is good, a blessing, and the tool needed to live out our dreams in a money world and pass financial success to our future generations. How we deliver our success is entirely up to us. Once we start growing into a meaningful journey, we will begin to see the world in a wholly new form. I hope this new world is a good vision for us.

How do we build ourselves into a meaningful purpose? A tool that is missed and skipped by many. I have watched students skip this all the time. I have ignored it. Why? I ignored it because I did not know my purpose; I found myself lost, and I was confused.

See, how the past created my reality? I did not know what my purpose was. The only thing I knew was I wanted better for my life. This is why I say, we need to witness our actions and understand that our history will direct our lives and our future if we do not take possession of our realities.

You may ask yourself at times why you react the way you do in certain situations. Can it be trauma? Or maybe it was the trauma that your ancestor experienced that built a traveling emotion, a saying, a belief, or energy that packaged itself and was delivered to your generation?

The Universe/God/mind called you to redirect this emotion, this sometimes hidden or blocked imprint, or you would have never picked up this book.

Something inside of you guided you to this book. It is up to you to finish this book and put this information in action to develop a higher you, and that higher you will reveal your meaningful purpose.

Many tools are out there in many books, which confuse people, especially those having the mindset of contently passing something up and moving to the next. I watch this with people. I call these people book, life coach, and certificate junkies. They will look for new coaches and/or certificate programs as an excuse that they are not ready and do not hold enough information to start. It is just another level of fear or lack of faith in themselves.

We must face a journey in life, or maybe that is only a limited belief. Why did I have the feeling money was not significant on this journey? Do I believe the secret of success can be dangerous in the wrong hands, yes? But, having this limited belief cannot hold back the good from advancing; it will almost be like taking away the right to self-defense from those that need it because of what evil people do. No longer can we punish or hold back the good from getting rich because of the greedy. Or the fear that greed will take over our lives. Another one of those limited beliefs. We need more good people who are financially wealthy than we need money-greedy people.

For years now, I have been drilling myself with Napoleon Hill's work. I found myself seeking a higher me and believing the money will find me, only to hold myself from building more. Yes, I had to learn through whatever time it took me to learn the lesson. But, I cannot say I am sitting here feeling that if I had more financial wealth, I could have advanced my learning faster. Yes, I question whether the journey made me good or always the right person looking to do good things. Perhaps I would have healed my mindset faster if I had focused more on making money than on learning more or focusing on debt. Or did I use that wisdom seeking, searching for answers as an excuse that I was not ready? Maybe deep down I feared cash in some form? If I did, was it my fear or someone else's? Or was it for control?

It is one thing to love money, but one can also fear wealth and reality. Some can fear a meaningful purpose. Some become workaholics as an excuse to stay away from family. Some can become over-consumed chasing secrets that hide the hidden truths deeper. Perhaps some become over-consumed in a spiritual journey. I believe that both purposes grow, and a meaningful purpose extends, and yes, both can drive you. My view is that a meaningful purpose guides you to a place you never dreamed about.

The purpose is like trying hard to attract something or some idea into our life. Imagine you are driving, looking for something healthy to eat. That is a purpose now, and suddenly, you are driving past fast-food restaurants—one after another. Now your mind starts to find reasons: Why not pull over and grab something fast? Maybe it would save me some time anyway. What harm can one meal do? I am strong; I can handle one unhealthy meal.

Let it known that billions upon billions of dollars are spent researching how the mind works and redirecting the thought. The saddest truth is, people's program is for quickness, fast, easy, secrets, mysteries. Every moment we go against the negative, and sometimes that drives our meaning. How do we filter out the negative? By building a positive outlook in life; this should be your purpose. And your actual hidden truth, your meaningful direction, will appear right in front of your eye when the mind is ready to see.

Yes, harmful temptations will be on this journey. In the beginning, for me, unhealthy temptations became my life, my purpose. I was not in control of my reasoning. Someone or something else was. And when someone else is in control, life starts to fade away; anger, anxiety, stress, and much more begin to fill the void. I became a slave to these sales tactics, limiting beliefs, ideas that took over my thinking. Someone else directed my life.

The hidden truth is learning how to direct your mind to reflect outward and accept a new vision. The original will find you. You do not have to spend your energy trying to chase a secret or go after a purpose, or give your life trying to attract something to you. All you must do is work on you every moment of your life. What tools you use is up to you. You are the hidden truth, and the truth reveals itself on the journey of self-healing and growing. Stop seeking! You have found your meaningful destiny!

4
Crisis to Riches

God wants us to be rich, and God shows us the way, and that way is in the journey. We are the story. We are the journey. Believing not in something greater, we become less of who we could be: God is the Divine Guide.

I am the word. I become the words that are after I am. Who are you? I am …

I hold all the answers that I seek. No one can hide the responses from me but myself. I search for the answers in books. I can read or hear what I allow my mind, or whatever the mind is, to witness. The hidden truth of success is in the mind and how you teach the mind to accept riches.

My question is, the crises that we need to overcome have been created by God or by the will of men and women? We all know humans designed the coronavirus. We all have habits and lifestyle patterns that created our realities. I would also question how many illnesses our life practices have built into reality. Our bodies can only work so hard, and boy, do we push it every day.

The mind is everything; the writings in this book should help open your mind, and I hope these writings will trigger a deeply hidden seed.

What happens is that we let the negative seeds grow. I know it is easier when everyone else is doing it. Maybe God put you there, or your will and actions put you there. How you got there is not the question. The question is, how to turn crises into riches?

It is time to grow up and grow into your dreams. You are a seed in the dirt, and you cannot wait for other sources to start developing, for you may spend a lifetime waiting for others.

It is your journey that you have been born to live out. You cannot look for others to do it for you. It is up to you to start cultivating yourself, because you are the seed to success.

Trauma to riches

Trauma feeds anger and hate, and when you are not in control of your emotions, someone else takes over. Trauma to wealth is controlling and transforming your emotions.

Before I was born, my family worried about my mother's health. My mother worried about her health and battled her health all of her life.

My mother conceived me when she was around twenty-seven years old. The doctors advised her that her heart was not healthy enough to give birth and that she should have an abortion. She decided to put me onto the Earth. She survived giving birth to me. My mother and I were inseparable until one day, when I was around two and a half, she vanished from my life. I can still see the vision alive in my mind in great detail. It is the only memory I have of her. I sat in the back seat in the car; she turned around, looked at me, and lit a cigarette. The final image that I have is of sitting in the vehicle's back seat in front of a brick building, watching my mother and dad walking into a building with a bag in hand.

My mother had diabetes as a child and battled with treatments. She passed at the age of thirty-one. In a child's mind, what had just happened—pain, suffering, abandonment, confusion. The subconscious took a major emotional blow, an imprint that helped create my reality.

My reality was building before I was born. My reality was born in my mother's womb and maybe long before that. My mother's emotional, worrying patterns got imprinted in my mind while I was most likely in her womb. The doctors said her heart was too weak to give birth to me, most likely killing her.

What was in my child's mind? Why did my mom leave me? Why did God take my mother away from me? Why me? Maybe even, what is wrong with me? I cannot tell you the real feelings I had. My mind did a fantastic job covering up that pain.

My mind pushed that memory far into the deep and covered up the pain. My subconscious wanted to protect me from that pain. My mother's death hit the entire family, and I ended up absorbing everyone else's emotional patterns. It was the death of my mother that set the ways for my family's life. I was the one that decided to learn how to face my traumas and teach myself how to take control and direct experience.

Before 2013 I did not believe in God. My dad did not believe in God; my child's emotions blamed God for taking my mother away. I probably blamed my mother for leaving me. Imagine the self-sabotage I had created in my life, the anger and hate that I built against myself, and how that reflected my reality. Why again, one must ignore attracting in the law of attraction at this time.

That is why when I wrote my first book, I called it *Self-Heal and Become Success*. As I was secretly developing into my definition of success, I was also healing and rewriting my past patterns. I was healing not only myself but also my ancestors' patterns from the beginning of time. I was rewriting my reflection that attracted my reality. What I wanted to attract into my life a few years ago is not the same as what I want to draw today. Labels and definitions drive people's dreams away.

Whose patterns created your reality? Whose dreams have you been chasing? Whose definition of success or life are you trying to attract into reality?

Some of you reading this may be triggering hidden emotions.

I was speaking once, and this lady from the audience told me that she was angry and that she hated him. I told her, "You need to know you are not alone in this world, and you holding onto the pain is not helping anyone. Mostly, it is not helping you. However wrong it was that happened to you, millions of people had it worse."

As painful as it was, my mother's death guided me to be the person I am today. That is a blessing. God blessed me, for He gave me a crisis/blessing that I have turned toward riches and assets. Holding on to the pain was not helping anyone else and mostly it was not helping me. It is a blessing that I could transform my pain into helping others.

In my lifetime, if I could change one person's life, all of my sufferings were worth it. I am blessed. But I did not only help one person. I know I have shifted many lives already, and this journey has only begun. That is power.

5

Strength of Forgiveness

The morning God spoke to me

Forgive me, Father, for I did not understand why I had to receive this trauma. Forgive me, Mother, for I did not understand that you had to leave me. Forgive me, Father, for I did not understand the power of being abandoned and alone. Forgive me, Father, for I did not understand my purpose. Forgive me, Father, for I let myself not recognize the gifts that I have received. Forgive me, Father, for I chose to dwell in pain. Forgive me, Father, for I allowed others to use my pain against me. Forgive me, Father, for denying you. Forgive me, Father, for I believed you left my side and abandoned me when you have been guiding me all of my life, like a proud dad and mom showing me the way to truth. Forgive me, Father, for not seeing and accepting your love. Forgive me, Father, for not recognizing how powerful you have made me. Forgive me, Father, for allowing disease, hate, anger, jealousy, greed, and all other negatives to live in my temple as I ignored your light, your guidance. Forgive me, Father, for I denied your healing. Forgive me, Father, for not knowing who I was and how powerful I am.

Forgive me, Father, for I turned my pain into anger. Forgive me, Father, for I denied your protection. Forgive me, Father, for rejecting Jesus. Forgive me, Father, for denying myself. I accept your guidance to become the light to the world. That is how powerful I am. I am that, that cannot be explained in names, stories, or labels. I am that, that can only shine the light through my reflection for the ones seeking the light. Amen.

Father, forgive them, for they know not what they do.
—Jesus

The text was a message one morning of an emotional clearing. I had reached a new level of healing and a new understanding of how powerful I am. Our strength can be endless if we only have faith in ourselves. Father, God, mind, Universe, Source, secret, self—the labels are continuous. Labels blind us, like believing in a secret or trying to attract or manifesting who we are not. Every brand is a guide to teach you about yourself. Did people blind us from this truth, or have we blinded ourselves? When was the last time you forgave yourself?

6

Definitions

The life we live is a repetition of our past generations. We buy motivation in other people's definitions of success. Are we chasing other people's meaning of life? Are our thoughts ours? The entire world's motivation is worthless if we never turn motivation into action, returning to our authentic dreams or our real purpose. Selling you to yourself holds the secrets to flourishing in life, the secrets of the law of attraction, or whatever label you choose.

Many seek other people's definition of wealth. Some attempt to find riches through motivators selling get-rich-quick ideas as a definition of success. You can jump up and down, get motivated all you want. Still, the moment you replace motivation with fear, you return to arguing with your other self, reflecting anger, frustration, and stress to yourself and your surroundings. Many become angry at their jobs, family members, friends, and others, leading themselves further and further away from genuine freedom. Deep down, they are mad at themselves; they have filled their thoughts with stress, anger, or any contrary deed. The mind can dwell in false emotions. Some may fall into a deep depression, manifest anxiety, or become physically ill.

Stress, anxiety, and depression are all signs that you live other people's success definitions as you become frustrated with allowing your dreams to fade away. I am not a doctor. I am just explaining my experience through my life transformation. (Always seek medical help if you feel you have lost control.)

The never-ending goal of seeking and creating the correct definition of success is hard work. Most will love the job because it guides those people back to the true self's path, their purpose in life, aligning them with the universal law. The most laborious work and the most significant battle that you will face is within yourself. Overcome everything that holds you back from who you are and reveal the precise definition of success.

Definitions, labels are all tools to explain something that cannot be defined. I had witnessed these definitions of labels exchanged from past generations and lived out in the present realm while passing them on to the future generations. Others cannot explain success as success is only described through experience during the journey returning to prosperity. Learning how to remove all human-made labels, ideas, definitions and returning to the accurate description of who you are is the key. I can sit down and write a title attempting to explain what I believe success is to me. I won't. You cannot define something that can only be described by experience. Many have tried.

I have spent most of my life chasing other people's definitions. At the same time, I kept giving myself excuses to not consider that I held the true meaning of life inside of me. I do not have the right to label the experience that you will witness on the journey of returning to self. It will only weigh you down longer.

My journey is not the same as anyone else's. Your life journey is your teacher. You can learn from your teacher or deny your teacher for the rest of your life. Your teachings are in your path of experience and will reveal themselves in the way. Most will dismiss their journey by arguing with their other self, looking for an effortless route to happiness. They do not listen to their other self and consequently restrain themselves from ever realizing the so-called secret to life's riches.

Influenced by my past, I developed a dependent mindset by listening to others tell me how I am supposed to live my life and how to survive. Living with a dependent attitude removed me from living with the free will of my thoughts. That guided me further and further away from who I honestly am. It forced me into living someone else's life—seeking money, seeking wealth, and blinding myself from an experience of thriving in wealth.

Losing free will to my thoughts forced me to give up on my dreams and forced me to live a life in my past generation's fears, frustrations, and hate and forget about the definition of success from my previous generations. Opportunities did not exist, and successful people become demonized.

When we live without free will, we live in our past, losing the passion for thriving. If we believe successful people are evil, then deep down, we will never seek success. It is not what you are worth that matters. It is what you do after you receive financial and life wealth that will lead you to the exact definition of success or destroy who you indeed are.

If you decide to take the road toward your purpose in life, you will have to jump into your journey one hundred percent. Do not worry if you do not know how. Just start at once. I will repeat, your journey will teach you if you open yourself to your life guides.

Guides will appear during your journey to teach you how to open the mind to new thoughts. The truth is, a closed mind closes doors, and when you start developing, your mind will be forced open. An open mind attracts the new, and a closed mind draws the same. An open mind opens other minds toward great wisdom. A closed mind slams the door shut to another person's knowledge. Those who are shortsighted will never get out of their own way.

The mind wants to connect with other like-minded people. The mind wants to grow by combining with another intelligence. Like attracts like. Open yourself to the gateway to universal consciousness. We seem to forget that our thoughts are what draw phenomenal wisdom.

We spend all our energy trying to attract the wrong into our lives, wearing a cloak—no wonder why we can never find real success in ourselves. We are seeking everything that we are not.

The real purpose of life is to find success within. Some will seek money and find true abundance from within. Many will work at attracting material wealth and overspend a lifetime living other people's definition of being rich and letting their conscience decay. Some will seek wealth and find an abundance of success while giving back, guiding others toward a life of divine riches.

You are who you are for a reason. Find that reason and

return yourself to a life of prosperity. Never let yourself dwell on the past. The past is only lessons guiding you to your real purpose in life.

We are worthy of receiving great abundance.

Self-development books
In this book, you will find many different definitions of the secrets to success and many descriptions of success; it may not come to you at once, and it may take years for you to recognize what the secret to success is.

> *The mind does not read self-development books.*
> *The mind develops into an understanding of the books.*

The mind, or the brain, or the thoughts can only see, recognize, and understand the level it knows and witnesses what it believes is correct. This is why some teachers say, you need to have emotions in it to attract. The mind needs a lot of stimulation at times. Remember, the thought does not know the difference between what is real and what is not; it wants to create.

Fake it until you make it, or lie to yourself until you start believing it. See how it works in a positive situation. In reverse, negative thoughts like the news media, everything negative, and medication commercials with repeated illnesses with side effects. The mind is mighty and very weak at the same time. If you are not in control, someone or something else is. Turn off the news. The media is a form of fear affirmations. Fear it until you believe it, become it, and buy it.

Definitions, labels, other people's ideas blind us. Let us take religion. We all defend the stories and do not understand the teachings of the words. Are the stories real or not? I do not know for sure, and I doubt anyone else knows. Do the stories explain the laws of life? If this is true, all, or most, stories teach you the hidden truths to success. Suppose you read books explaining something in story form. You will find the books teach life patterns for the life journey or lifestyle patterns.

All texts guide us through stories about how to overcome the stages of our life. However, I stopped seeing words, labels, and names and understood that all books try to explain something that words cannot describe. Also, people see other people's journeys at the level of their mindset, which is why we have great brilliant books showing you the story in more than one vision or explanation.

It is essential to understand the answers we seek are not located in the books; our descriptions are from our level of our belief, and one will find that what one desires is situated in the mind at the level of mindset. Yes, as you grow, the words you read develop.

There are tools for directing our desires, and in reverse, they are the tools for leading ourselves negatively.

The tools used to reveal the secret to success in reverse are the tools to direct others negatively. The mental devices in the right hands can be great for societies, and the mystery in the wrong hands can be destructive.

Good vs. evil, negative vs. positive, anger vs. happiness, and on and on. All are real, and there is a battle for your mind. Remember, some people live unhealthy lifestyles, and positive people live more of a healthier lifestyle; sometimes the negative person believes they are living a happy lifestyle.

Are you living a harmful lifestyle, or are you looking at having a lot of money that allows you to live an unhealthy lifestyle?

Have you ever heard the line: What you focus on you become?

We must seek balance in life, not only focus on money. Lifestyle is everything. If you want to change your world—or anyone else's world—you must shift everything about yourself and about them, building lifestyles, not just the bank accounts.

If we do not focus on all of us, well, you can figure out what will happen. But the one thing you will need to become rich financially and in life is productive time and energy. We all know someone that focused their entire life on making money and lost everything else—rich in the pocket and living in poverty of the mind.

7

Transforming Reality

We seek and seek for something that will make us rich quickly. We are programmed to search for easy money, which causes us to work harder while consuming ourselves, making others rich, and jumping from one idea to another. One coach to the next. One book to the next.

Coronavirus of 2020 became a significant asset. When you focus on success, you start to create success. Even though I am trained to control my thoughts and direct my success, I still found myself seeing the words "Corona Virus" run in my head every time I shut my eyes. I tried my hardest to shut off the news and hide all posts on social media. I do this for anything that may direct my energy, beliefs, or energy negatively. I also have to admit that I knew a lot more about coronavirus because my sister was on the frontline, being a nurse in a hospital.

My mind had come a long way from the world I used to know.

Every adversity, every failure, every heartbreak, carries with it the seed of an equal or greater benefit.
—Napoleon Hill

A pandemic helped guide me into a deeper understanding of the proof that the world will direct your success, if you only learn how to shift your thinking or how you see a situation. The Earth/Universe/God will also guide you to your failure if that is the place you choose to focus on. Many unknowingly lead themselves to defeat or self-destruction because of a hidden imprint in mind. Or some negative or weakening belief—a seed that has grown like a weed.

Seeds can be immensely powerful; when I talk of a seed, I am speaking of a thought, a belief that you allow to grow and grow. Maybe into forests. What if I told you that by planting positive reviews of what you desire, you could start to shift your entire life?

One of the most astounding restricted beliefs is that the answers we seek are outside of us, guiding many toward a life of seeking. This is exactly why seeking a secret is a fool's journey—also the reason why some need to be tricked into traveling toward understanding the great tools of success. Yes, my friends, we also tend to jump from one success instrument to the next in the hope of finding some secret to achieve magical success. If you understand this, you can sell to these kinds of people over and over. I have witnessed people get pumped up at what I call a "pump a rally" and hand over their retirement into some investing or business ideas.

I almost lost a big chunk of my 401k investing in real estate notes. I lent this money as a hard lender. I was the bank for this property. I never paid attention to my account. I figured a self-directed IRA was like my 401k and was looked over by someone else.

The investor never paid the taxes and walked away from the property.

In December I paid taxes on some land that I had picked up "Land Banking." I found a note on the investment note. When I called in and asked about this message, I found out the investor had walked away from the investment in March of that year. Now the panic kicked in, as I figured the house must be destroyed, abandoned for eight months without insurance. I was ready to give up and walk away and felt I had been screwed and robbed.

I have to admit I was way out of my comfort zone. I was petrified and angry that I spent all those years building my 401k to turn into a self-directed IRA. I felt I was scammed and deceived.

The property was fifteen hours away. The news media was talking very negatively about this area. I had no idea about investing in my state, let alone out of state. The negative thinking was strong and powerful. I also wanted to walk away from this problem. It was the easiest thing to do at the time. Heck, it was retirement money, and I could not touch it anyway, so the mindset made it feel like it was not my money.

> *Opportunity often comes disguised in the form of misfortune or temporary defeat.*
> —Napoleon Hill

Being trained in the philosophy of Napoleon Hill's PMA (positive mental attitude) Science of Success and teaching myself through action how to put PMA into my own life, and writing my book allowed me to take control of my focus, emotions, and thoughts.

I said to myself, "I am turning this scary financial situation into a positive one." PMA or positive mental attitude, accurate thinking, master mind alliance, creative vision, and applying faith are a few of Napoleon Hill's principles that I pulled out to work for me.

Being the owner of an air-conditioning and heating company, writer on self-development, and a Napoleon Hill Foundation certified leader and instructor helped me build an extensive network of business owners, coaches, mentors, and investors. I got to know Carl Schiovone (www.CarlSchiovone.com), a mentor who runs East Coast Real Estate Investors Association, a networking group that I belong to on Long Island, New York. Being able to pick up my phone and give Carl a call helped guide me with some answers that I needed to seek out.

I contacted all those connected to my IRA, and with the right questions and attitude, I was able to get someone to look at the property for free. I had faith. Everything would be OK. I received photos of the property, and the inside of the house was spotless and ready to rent. I said to myself, "Thank you, God." Clicking on the next picture revealed a cross with Jesus on the wall. If that is not a sign, I do not know what to tell you.

One more thing—in 2013, I did not believe in God or any higher power. I did not believe in myself. Over time, developing my life, I learned to understand that something powerful exists. Something extraordinary is guiding me, and to the best of my belief, I think it is impossible to explain what I have been witnessing with words, and I believe many have tried—holding down many.

I also belong to an organization, and I was able to reach out to someone in the property area, and he just so happened to be a real estate investor. I was able to get my hands on local contacts and all the information on the location. A blessing or years of manifestation?

The foreclosure process started, and that was when I found out about the back taxes and that the town would auction off the property in three months if the taxes were not up to date. My IRA account had to pay the taxes on a property, and I did not own it yet.

The moral of this story is I could have turned this into a self-crisis from which someone else would have profited. As I visited the home and talked to other investors and contractors working on the same block, they told me that investors were all over that house. They wanted it.

As I was trained to take control of the mind, I could shift a situation. I controlled my mind and emotions and saw the light on the other side of the tunnel. I transformed what could have been a crisis into riches.

Was this magic? In some eyes, maybe? But I had to control and direct the mind; then I had to travel toward the light at the other side of the tunnel, and I had to overcome everything that was in the way, including myself. I will say the wisdom from it, and the guidance, felt like magic or as if a higher power was guiding me.

OMG, can the secret to success be the law of God? But if

it is, how does one explain it to someone else without turning them off? I guess for those that may get turned off the second you say, God, we will trick them somehow. Maybe we can call God's law as universal law or law of attraction. How about we call it a secret message?

8

Message

With what you already possess, how can you create more financial wealth and freedom?

Like many others, we look outside of ourselves for answers. We rarely take an inventory of our life and the assets life has already provided us. It is almost like we have throwaway dreams and assets. Today, everything is replaceable once we get bored, and maybe our consumer mindsets are pushing us away from success.

I sat down one day, and I thought about what was holding me down. Yes, I wanted to coach people, but I could not give away my wisdom for free. No one was interested. I have learned not to give away my skills and insight for free because I have put in the time and earned it to make money; moreover, almost no one appreciates anything given free.

Once I received it, I understood the message, "With what I already possess, how can I create more financial wealth and more freedom to live out my desires?"

It told me that I have to focus on all that I know and start building from there. See, even when you put the work in and level up, you find another layer of excuses that prompt you to look outward.

If you look back in time and see how your life guided you this far, you can see the steps needed toward your meaningful purpose. Eventually, you will understand that we repeat generations with the same patterns. The world is waiting for the ones who will shift those patterns. Sometimes we need to build one platform to reach the next.

One tool to manifesting ideas, information, and guidance is to imprint something in your mind. What did I do? I have been working on this for years, and I have worked with many tools.

One tool I use is sticky notes around the house to remind my mind to remind me what I am working for every day.

Second, I have whiteboards and green dry-erase markers. I write out what I want in life, and I keep it somewhat simple on the whiteboard. I also have a future wall on which I have put up pictures of my fundamental goals.

Most times when I received a message, I did not know the meaning of what I received at that time. However, I had faith that I would grow into the answers as long as I kept the idea, vision, or question alive in my mind. No, you do not have to focus on any of it. You only need to remind the mind in a way that works for you.

In big green letters on my whiteboards, one at the entrance of my office and the other one at the door at my house that I walk in and out of every day, I wrote, "With what I already possess, how can I create more financial wealth and more freedom to live out my desires?"

You may ask, why green? It reminds me of money because I finally faced the fact that if I want to impact my life and others in the money world, I must first have the finances to do so.

At first, I would walk past the question every day, and one day like magic, I understood the guidance.

Before this question came to me, I and the rest of the Global Team had canceled the March 21st New York event. Due to the risk of COVID-19, New York went into lockdown on March 22nnd. I was upset because I had just overcome my fear of public speaking and traveling last year and had started speaking globally, and now everything had come to a standstill.

Not only did the message guide me, but COVID's lockdown showed me the answer. I said to myself, "I am unbelievable at troubleshooting the air-conditioning system." I had an "essential" business, and I could not travel. What did I do? I focused 100 percent on the air-conditioning company, and I worked every day that I could. I pretty much worked seven days a week, twelve to sixteen hours a day for months straight. I was focused and determined. I had nothing else to do anyway with the lockdown in place. Boy, was I blessed with the amount of work I received. When you are focused, determined, and willing to work hard at it, the blessings/ abundance spirals its way toward you.

I put a wall around me. I stopped seeking outside of me, and I returned to what I already possessed. I evaluated my past and what had guided me this far. I also shifted my mindset and realized my life had trained me already. The skills I had accumulated in the heating and air-conditioning trade. That moment was when my energy changed and grew. That was the moment my manifestation and attraction were the strongest.

When you look at your job or business as a vessel, your energy shifts; we are on a ship guiding us to our next level. You do not have a job. You are on a vessel.

1. Evaluate your vessel and ask yourself how you can create more wealth and remember this. It may be baby steps. Even a seventy-five-cents-an hour raise would be a great start. See what is happening now? You are starting to focus on creating more with what you already have. You are raising your value. I believe this may guide you faster than jumping all over the place. The quicker you learn to focus, the faster what you focus on will reveal itself.

    For example, my business is heating and air-conditioning, and I loved speaking and teaching life development. I wanted to coach others. I had a mind shift when I looked at my business to create wealth and look for ways to run the business more by itself. Why could I not take some time and build a self-sustainable business? So I could live my dreams speaking and teaching around the world—this built excitement and motivated me to work harder at my company.

    I have built this vessel for years now. It took me years to receive licenses to work all over Long Island. I created a strong customer base. I spent years weeding out cheap and wrong customers, the ones that

are takers. Character attracts character. The more I grew, more the level of my customers grew.
2. Evaluate again.

I started to look into residual income. First, I thought about getting into real estate. Again looking outside of my vessel, I began to look at my business/vessel as real estate. This made me focus on selling yearly contracts. Why would I spend all this time working on real estate when I could with absolutely no effort provide contracts? Not only was it effortless but I also had customers beg me to sell the contracts. See, I build my character every moment in life and business, and this made me stand out over others, and my customers wanted me and my service, and they wanted me to guaranty I would come to them when they called.

I want to tell you a story about when the idea of the vessel tactics came to me. I was speaking for Amanda at Think and Grow Rich Sweden. One of the students talked about their job and did not look to quit their job yet. For now, it was a side idea and the student was not ready to jump in 100 percent. Also, this was the person who told me about the Jante Law.

I understand the fear of jumping in 100 percent as most coaches will tell you that you have to jump in 100 percent, as accurate as this may be. We must understand the fear and limiting beliefs before finding the courage to walk away from a secure job. My understanding of fear made me recognize that I could tell this person that they need to jump in 100 percent and walk away from the job, or I could guide that person in a way that would build confidence.

Which idea do you think will do more for most people? Keep in mind that this person was already very successful in life.

Personally, it took me years and two side business failures to find the courage to walk away from my secure union job. Even when I was ready to quit the job, I found myself walking into the office and walking out without giving my two weeks' notice. I repeated this for months before I found the courage to give my two weeks' notice.

I and others are walking away from everything they know to enter the unknown. So the advice to jump in 100 percent or shock my students with curse words is disrespectful and foolish. For some, jumping in 100 percent is not an option yet, and I would never want someone to walk away from a chance of developing into what it takes to leap 100% into the unknown.

We must plant the seed, not push people away. We need to be a helping hand. When the time is right, the world will open up to you.

The fear of the unknown is one of the greatest fears you need to overcome. No one is going to do it for you. Only you can face the unknown, and the tool you need is action. Action is the place that reveals the next levels. We tend to seek comfort zones and security blankets in others for confidence.

I helped to shift this person's thoughts. I said: "Do not look at your job as a job. The job is a vessel getting you to whatever you desire." What does this do? It excites you. It may even remove unwanted pressure and/or some forms of anxiety about your present and future. (I am not a doctor. All I did was explain through my experiences.) Your thoughts are no longer stale. The mind starts to learn how to develop and seek a new direction. You have just pulled the anchor, and you are on the way to building more faith in the flow of life. You may not even recognize it, but these minor shifts can start the journey of confidence-building.

9

Law of Accepting

Law of attraction. We have all heard of this one. Wow, powerful. It sounds like all we need to do is attract, and attracting must be easy. I wonder how many people get excited hearing those words "law of attraction" and dabble with some so-called teachers and give up on their dreams. Yes, the law of attraction is real, but as I stated in my book *Self-Heal and Become Success*, you need to ignore the "attraction" in the law of attraction.

Many people think they can find success if they create a vision board and put up a picture on a wall of what they want, and like magic, the attraction will answer. I too ask you to do those things, yes, but be sure to use them as your tools. Add any tools you believe that can help guide you. Remember, what tools work for you may not work for me or others. As long as you are opening the mind and developing, you will be growing the attraction in the law of attraction.

Why would I tell my readers to ignore the attraction in the law of attraction? I hope you are getting an understanding. What do I mean, you ask. If you are chasing someone else's ideas, beliefs, or definitions, you will attract that into your life in some form.

One of the most powerful tools I use to shift what I accept into my life is the words I speak and how I define something.

Do not think big. Think bigger.

I have spent years trying to attract. I worked hard toward what I wanted, envisioned it, begged the Universe, hung pictures up, created affirmations. But, nothing, no magic. Why? Because deep within, I did not accept it into my life, and for good reasons, I am glad I did not, for I was creating hidden emotions, societies, and past generation's beliefs into reality.

Ignore trying to attract and let the attraction come to you.

I have watched many people spend all their energy focusing on things and people not needed in their journey. If you beg the Universe for an ex back, ask why the Universe separated that relationship in the first place. Sometimes we need to have trust in our journey even at our deaths.

Internal trauma, past patterns, hidden and covered-up beliefs, and past successes created who we are today and what we have accepted into our reality. I named my first book *Self-Heal and Become Success* and my website Returning2success.com is what I believe the place the law of accepting reveals itself. We start returning to our passions. We begin to unmask our meaningful purpose.

Ideas and definitions of success from others begin to fade away.

The mind starts opening toward the road that begins to reveal a meaningful purpose.

The mental argument starts taming itself.

These laws are natural laws and can be shifted, developed, and directed to benefit us, and we can stop fighting against ourselves. Yes, the fight within is real.

The mind starts teaching us how to control both worlds: the inner world and the outer world.

The most important thing for this law is character attracts character. Once you can embrace this, you start to grow or self-heal your way to prosperity. What do I mean? We are a reflection, and we accept or attract that reflection, right? Your friends, your surroundings, have almost all the same characters and beliefs, and you all pretty much attract or get the same reality. Right? So, the most straightforward tool is to witness and outdo the "yesterday you" in everything you do. Focus on the level of your moral character because that is what you accept as reality. You are the law of the law of attraction or the law of accepting.

You, the law/character, will grow, reflect outward, and will return to you in some form.

New levels—I am talking about new people, new beliefs, a new vision of the world, new levels of purpose. You will grow everything and everyone you know. You can choose to stay on a level, or you can very well develop into new groups for the rest of your life, I believe.

How do I use character to create more money? First off, the level of your character becomes the level of your customer—law of attraction. When I began my HVAC business, I was scared of many things. I procrastinated. I did almost everything on a negative scale. I built massive debt as an excuse that I was not ready and feared looking at my books. In the beginning, I did anything I could do just to get by. I guess I still had the paycheck to paycheck mindset.

But I was paying myself and putting the material on credit cards. Let's say, I maxed out within the first year of my business, ignoring my finances, listening to others how much I should charge, buying material wrong, making bad estimates, and still having the spending habits and lifestyle I had when I received a union paycheck with endless overtime.

I almost put myself out of business. Through the years, I started to change whom I accepted into my life. It was easy because as one grows, the law of accepting also becomes the law of repelling.

Opportunities

Opportunities are begging for acceptance because opportunities need your success to form into reality. I consider opportunities are souls that cannot take human form and can only experience reality through the actions of human beings.

Opportunities will help you grow. Options are blessings sent to you from the spiritual realm.

Opportunities are energy without physical form.

Opportunities are ideas without the ingredient of action.

When you realize you have the best life partner, your life becomes an asset, a blessing.

10

Lonely Road to Success

For me, the road to success has been lonely, and I will tell you it had to be. We are about to dig deeper into the law of attraction, the law of accepting, and the law of repelling.

What happens when we advance our character and advance who we are? We grow our attraction. Let me explain what happens, and to understand this better, we will use the laws as energy. Remember the level of your life will change what you accept or attract.

Your energy status will start to repel who and what does not belong on your journey; you have decided to grow, and others have not, and this may even happen in a relationship or marriage. The connection starts fading away little by little.

It does not fade away. One chooses to grow, and one decides to stay in the same realm. The energy no longer mixes. The growing one realizes they have been held down for a long time and most likely recognizes that it has been going on for generations. That lifestyle no longer interests the person in the growth mode.

The one not in growth may attack and try to bring down the one in development. The one who is developing, the one that became a seeker, is breaking from the comfort zone and stepping into the unknown. Comfort zones are hard for many to move out of.

The things, ideas, and people you enjoyed in the past start fading away. You get tired of arguing and debating with others, for you find it drains you, and your vision of success is growing. The repelling has begun, and you are now entering a new level.

Now, this is the part why many will find themselves alone on their journey. Your mind had not developed enough; that is it—that is the secret; that is the law of attraction, law of accepting, the law of repelling, and the law of receiving. No magic at all! Your mind has developed, and its vision and senses have grown. It may even feel like a new world has been formed in front of your eyes.

What you focus on, you grow into, or as others say, you become.

Now the lonely part—I call this in between levels. Remember those that repelled from you; you stopped seeing mind to mind or eye to eye with them. Now you have not developed enough to recognize or accept the next level of people that need to open to you with knowledge from the next level needed to advance you.

An open mind opens other's mind; a closed mind closes other's minds. It is so simple to see, but the work may be hard only because of the fight within and the fears.

When you are ready, the mind will open to a new level, and that mind will recognize fresh minds at new levels. Many people will explain this as if you think of a blue car, you will see blue cars. It is not that we are attracting it; we recognize it, and after we realize it, we must accept it.

It is not that the information is not in front of us. We deny the information we seek. The level of thought keeps one down, and until the person can see and accept the next level, the doors stay shut in the mind's eye.

Sometimes we cannot see because we are too busy in our minds. Therefore, it is easier to control people when their minds are occupied by other people and objects and false dreams and beliefs.

If you think you are losing everything, shift your focus, and you just may find yourself finding everything.

11

The Spiraling Effect

The spiral effect has three levels: downward, idle, or upward. All levels can be controlled or can run on autopilot. I hope to show you how to turn a downward or idle spiral into an upward spiral because it is critical to find a way to enjoy our lives without just spending all our time building.

We have all heard of the hitting rock bottom to success stories.

While listening to stories, many listen to the parts they want to hear. We never recognize the small steps that someone takes that keep them falling backward. One cannot hit rock bottom without having a downward spiral effect. The downward spiral has to have a starting point. Something has to trigger this downward shift, and it digs deeper and deeper. For many, this is their law of accepting unhealthy lifestyles. Something or someone took possession of their thinking.

I had control for most of my life, I believe, but little by little, the power or happiness started depleting away, and the downward spiral had begun. First, I lived the life—I worked out, had ripped abs, practiced martial arts, was successful at my union job, went clubbing on the weekends, went dancing, and dated many women. My life was remarkable.

One day one of my friends started with painkillers, and when painkillers became more challenging for him to get, it grew into heroin. I remember this friend showing me a full-page article in a magazine about how painkillers were heroin. It might as well have been be a heroin ad. Within a month, his life had spiraled out of control, and he disappeared from my life. The drug was too powerful for him.

At that moment, I felt like I had lost one of my closest friends. I tell you, it scared the hell out of me. It was probably the first time I ever witnessed someone losing control of their lives as a drug took over everything. It happened so fast.

Sometime after that heartache, I decided to stop training in martial arts in Brooklyn. I believed I needed a change in my life and I thought traveling into Brooklyn was too much. I guess my mind was well into creating this spiral toward rock bottom.

Following that training in martial arts, training on Long Island, I cracked my ribs; at this time, I was in the best shape of my life. I was eating correctly and working out every day.

On a job working in the mall every morning, I would walk to the other side of the mall to pick up an egg white and roast beef or turkey on whole wheat bread and walk to McDonald's, where the rest of the workers ate pancakes.

One morning I decided to treat myself to one pancake. I said it could not hurt me. What can one pancake do? I work hard, and I deserve a treat.

Before that job ended, I was eating full McDonald's breakfasts, and let's say I lost my abs fast. Again, another level of the spiral unwitnessed by me and that took over my life in autopilot mode. The eating habit took over.

Sometime after that, my dad died. Death had never bothered me before. My dad had made me tough on death, as he said work comes before funerals.

My dad's death hit this grown man like a ton of bricks. He was my best friend, and every day we practically worked at my house together.

The doctors had informed my mother that her heart was too weak for giving birth to me at the age of twenty-nine. My mother said she wanted to put me into this world, and she did. My mother survived giving birth to me and lived for another two and a half years. Then one day, she vanished from my life, disappeared. That last moment is still a robust, detailed vision in my mind today.

I believe my dad's passing triggered some childhood emotions, trauma from my mother passing when I was two and a half years old. The next level of the downward spiral began.

Following that was the fast-spinning downward spiral that started growing my eating and drinking alcohol cravings, as I was stressed out of my mind sitting in three to six hours a day in bumper-to-bumper traffic. I hated my life, was angry at the world, suffered anxiety and panic attacks, and almost blacked out at times, thinking I had a heart attack.

Now to understand this downward drop, you need to understand this did not happen in weeks or months. It was years in the making.

I always said to myself, "What happened to me? I was supposed to be so much more."

There is no way my mom risked her life to put me in this world for me to live a miserable life. I must have been put on Earth for a reason.

Now I was at the point in 2013, when I believe my mind went into survival mode. The beginning of my life development journey. The beginning of my first book, *Self-Heal and Become Success*.

It was in 2013 that my mind introduced me to self-development. The search for success had begun; only for me, survival looked a lot like my dreams of running a business, owning a Lamborghini, and driving to nightclubs to pick up stripper-type women. My definition of being rich at that time.

Therefore, I named my book *Self-Heal and Become Success*. While seeking the book title, I realized that all these self-development teachers, chasing a secret, trying to attract and manifest taught me how to self-heal myself and self-heal my thinking. At that moment, I realized I was always "success." I was not a success. I was not becoming successful, for I am "success" and always had been. I just needed to stop looking and start returning to my home, my desires, my definition of success—whatever that may be.

I had heard of some secret to riches. So the search began. At the same time, I created my HVAC business But searching for a secret sounded easier, so I spent a lot of my energy and years focused on a secret as an excuse not to build or focus 100 percent on my business and life. Who wants to work hard if there is some secret that makes you magically rich?

I wanted to know the secret to attract money.

It is easy to allow others to sell you your excuses if you are confused or have no one to ask for advice, or you are in fear and living with the habit of procrastination.

See, what I have found was I was spiraling into seeking something outside of me. Something that does not exist. In one book that I read and one movie I watched at the beginning of my journey, the speakers repeated the words "secret" continually, causing me to believe in a mystery. One day I am going to count how many times they say that word.

Remember, the mind wants to play with us, and what we repeatedly hear we become in some form. The problem, I realized, was I had wasted years and thousands upon thousands of dollars believing some magical secret to riches existed.

I realized I was the secret. I was the law of attraction. I was seeking, and I found it in the journey of bettering myself in life and business and studying extremely hard to get certified as a Napoleon Hill PMA Science of Success leader/instructor.

Therefore, chasing a secret outside of yourself is a fool's journey. It fooled me, and I used a mystery as an excuse I was not ready, which caused me to procrastinate my success.

Is the starting point of the spiral downward significant? No, you do not need to witness when the spiral downward started.

Maybe the downward spiral started at my birth. Perhaps the downward spin began in my mother's womb, Perhaps that spiral started generations and generations ago.

Yes, I am telling you that your level of the law of accepting can be from the beginning of time, and without self-healing those past patterns, the generation repeats and repeats in some form.

When we can see our journey connecting the dots backward, we can realize all those steps that developed the negative spiraling effect from which, for some reason, most cannot dig their way out.

Looking backward after discovering a new level of happiness during my journey, I can see all the steps that guided me to understand my success. I can see the work I put into myself and how I focused myself out of my spiral downward unconsciously.

The mind can work for you or against you. The mind can be your greatest asset.

Action forward or action backward or stale and idle are all a level of a state of mind and can be one's definition of success. Sometimes people deep down want to fail or want conflicts or any self-destructive effects. It is their definition of success or life. Negative fills their void.

The path one travels in the mind is the path in some form one travels in reality. The question is, why will many not recognize this spiral toward rock bottom? Because it happens very slowly, and it takes over.

A broken childhood or relationship or anything that may be a force of negativity, anger, hate, or anything harmful can occupy one's mind, which will also get transferred to one's reality in some form.

How do we trigger a shift that can dig us out of the downward spiral of rock bottom? If you hit rock bottom, you have nothing else to lose, so the climb outward begins.

You ask, do you have to hit rock bottom to become

successful? NO! That is why I am writing this book. I hope to guide you through a shortcut to success, and that is being aware of your actions. I do not want others to feel how I felt when I was alone and not knowing that I was addicted to a harmful life-style that caused me to drop into a downward spiral mentally and physically. That is why I put my story out into the Universe.

It may not be easy at first, but in time you should find your reality shift almost instantly.

- We need to let go of everything that holds us down.
- You are not to blame yourself.
- Witness your actions, your life.
- Make conscious decisions as if everything depends on it. For it does.
- Remember, character attracts character. Always witness all your actions.

The past is the past. Do not dwell in the past. To shift a negative spiral, we need to let the past fade away into the past.

When you find yourself spiraling downward or when you see things not going the way they should, stop and say to yourself, "What is that I am doing? I am the one that controls my reality." Start to shift your thoughts back on track and redirect your focus positively.

It may take practice. In time you should be able to shift your situation instantly, almost like magic. Is it a magic trick? No, you moved what your mind chooses to see, and the mind wants to gift you. OK, you just changed your focus, and your mind's eye sees the situation as a positive, no longer a negative. You are shifting the law of accepting.

Want to change someone's world? Shift the direction of their thinking. The mind does not understand the difference between destruction or success, and the mind wants to play with you. Let us play the game of creating financial wealth.

12

Guide of Divine

The beliefs of others seem to have created our lives.

This chapter will show you that many cannot get past the title, names, and labels.

I will also say, watch out for those that are demonizing others and beliefs.

Many people have tried to hide or explain the law of life by many different names and labels. They are all one law with various brands.

I am that. What words cannot reveal? I can only be described through the experience living my journey within the flow of Nature's/universal living law.

Many people have tried explaining with words and blinded many into chasing other people's definitions of what life is—causing many to spend their life experiences comfortable living in other people's definitions of success and happiness.

Let us tap into these laws; first off, remove all definitions and open the mind. Let us go back to the beginning of wisdom.

Throughout the world, we come across several texts and teachings. But for some reason, people love mysteries and stories about seeking treasure. Maybe it is in our DNA to find a lot of gold and money. Or perhaps we are programmed this way on purpose. Believe me. Many will pay a fortune of money and time to play mental and physical treasure hunting games. Remember, the more the mind seeks, the deeper is the game the mind creates.

It seems our minds are mighty, and we see now that our minds are the creators of our realities and the foundation of the future; and to change anything is to change what your mind accepts as reality.

We must direct our future generation toward success. If you can focus in that direction, rewards will return and develop in the mind, and the bank.

Money loves action.

Money is energy.

Our moral beliefs, religious beliefs, and beliefs about life are only a level of our mental state, our mental attitude, and our character. One must strive to cultivate a positive mental attitude that will redirect every challenge we face.

If the mind is programed only to see the positive in everything, the world around the mind will only accept an optimistic outlook. This positive mental attitude or mindset will always look past the negative and will always look for a positive direction. No matter how bad the situation is or how the movement of thoughts, beliefs, and energy is, the mind will accept only the positive. Like attracts like.

When we look at all these teachings, we find that all the

instructions guide us in one direction, and that direction is the direction one faces and directs action.

One can read and direct life with a negative mindset, or one can read and direct life with a positive mindset.

If you are not growing, you are dying.

Why do we demonize labels? Better yet, ask who taught us how to hate and become angry at other people's belief systems or definitions?

Like all self-development and religious instructions, everything in life, including our mindsets, has levels that spiral upward or downward.

We do not read self-development books. We grow into developing the understanding of these great books, and our self-development is the level of our minds. We have to remove the labels, open our minds, and create our definitions. We become the level of the description we believe.

Those who learn to control the definition of the world, rule the world.

Are people looking to hide God's laws that guide us to any level of reality our minds can create? I do not know if people look to suppress these great universal laws or read the rule wrong or deny them altogether.

If we never grow, the words stay the same.

For many, it is not the fear of failing but the fear of succeeding.

Maybe one does not want to leave the others behind.

One night I had a dream while I was researching and seeking the secret to success. I asked in my dream about the secret to success hidden in plain view. My dream advised me that the secret is not hidden and is in direct sight for all to read.

Then I asked if the American foundation is part of the secret to success, and my dream told me that the Founding Fathers understood the hidden truth about winning, and they shared the wisdom and teachings freely for the world to grow.

I woke up like I always wake up when I receive vital guiding information in my dreams. Like all my dreams and great teachers, they never give you the exact answer, and you have to do some research, or you need to grow into understanding the information you have received.

I said to myself, "Can it be described in the Constitution, a guide toward understanding the secrets toward success?" At that moment, I decided to look up the Declaration of Independence.

What did I find?

"When in the course of human events, it becomes necessary for one people to dissolve the political bands which have connected them with another, and to assume among the powers of the earth, the separate and equal station to which the Laws of Nature and of Nature's God entitle them, a decent respect to the opinions of mankind requires that they should declare the cause which impel them to the separation. We hold these truths to be self-evident, that all men are created equal, that they are endowed by their Creator with certain unalienable Rights, that among these are Life, Liberty and the pursuit of happiness...

We therefore, the Representatives of the United States of America, in General Congress, Assembled, appealing to the Supreme Judge of the world for the rectitude of our intentions, do, in the Name, and by Authority of the good people of these Colonies, solemnly publish and declare, That these

United Colonies are, and of Right ought to be, Free and Independent States; …

And for the support of this Declaration, with a firm reliance on the protection of divine Providence, we mutually pledge to each other our Lives, our Fortunes and our sacred Honor." -https://providenceforum.org/story/declaration-of-independence/

It was right in front of my eyes—the guide of the mind. God, The Divine Providence, and I realized why I could not understand the secrets. I denied GOD, I refused success, and I looked for strength outside of me—restraining myself and my calling. It was my upbringing, and I, probably as a kid, blamed God for taking my mother. I may even have witnessed my dad and siblings losing faith in God.

Strength comes from the inside. We need to accept the energy to recognize power. We must feel it to believe it. But if we are spiritual or energy beings, we are downplaying ourselves or letting others lower our standards. Thinking is only half the strength. Living it and applying action is the other half. That is when faith is born. Reading for the rest of your life and ignoring the tools, never putting the writings into action is of no use. We are too busy begging for comfortable lives, without ever understanding; that if we apply action, we will figure it out faster and the quicker we will be free.

We have all heard the Ten Commandments. But, we cannot direct those few golden rules of life. No, we keep searching for the treasure. If you want to hide something from someone, hide it right in front of them. We seem to have the habit of making things extremely hard for ourselves.

Why do we chase others' ideas instead of ours? Because we set ourselves to fail with the tool of blaming others. Once you realize that, you will have to take full responsibility for your actions when you start to find your way toward you. Are you done lettings others sell your excuses to you? I know I am.

The Ten Commandments

No other gods before me.
We are one with God and God lives through us. It is we that need to live out our meaningful purposes. I believe God is that hidden drive within guiding us on our journey. This hidden drive should be your only guide. This drive took years of development for me to recognize it. It is like your purpose is clouded, and a force is pushing you forward. You do not know why, but after all of your argument, you came to trust this feeling, for it never guided you wrong, and it drove you past what you believed is your purpose and guiding you to a place you never envisioned. At first, I wanted to copy others' images, but I returned 2 success, I returned to me, and I found a new piece of art, not like anyone else's I know. I discovered my meaningful purpose, and that is myself.

You shall not make for yourself a carved image.
Never become someone else's image, even God's. We already had an idea, a seed planted into us. We are all created equal with this seed, a meaningful purpose. The law of Nature is growth. But, many will spend a lifetime trying to copy those we are not supposed to be.

You shall not take the name of the Lord your God in vain.
The Supreme Being is powerful, and a belief without action or belief empty or meaningless without applying faith into action is the same as all talk and no action. Nature wants to grow. The Universe rewards those with success, the ones that take action in their lives. God is energy, confidence, strength, power; Guide of Divine is the secret ingredient of life's riches. Don't just read the philosophy; become it, and don't let others define it for you. Only you hold the definition of your Guide.

Remember the Sabbath day.
Rest and appreciate your hard work. Burning out is real and weakens one's drive. When was the last time you witnessed Almighty's great job? The mind needs time to declutter. If we never shut down, we can never file our thoughts and will miss some extraordinary inner guidance. Remember, the most successful people have found success in silence or in Nature, which is why they allow their minds to rest.

Honor your father and your mother.
How you treat others, authority, or the laws given is how you treat yourselves. It is a reflection of who you are. Respect the rules and respect yourself. Character attracts character. Honor even those who do not honor you, for honoring others is honoring yourself.

You shall not murder.
Sadly, this rule must be included here; we should all know the haunting of the mind that we will have to deal with,

looking over one's shoulders for the rest of life. But, I would like to look at it from another outlook. How many dreams have been murdered by others? Have you destroyed other people's confidences with negativity? Every action, every word has a rippling effect. Everyone is setting rippling effects forward.

You shall not commit adultery.
I am currently single. I am leaving this one alone, and I will leave it to your imagination.

You shall not steal.
Do not take from others, get what you are worth that you earned, and never take more than you deserved. Remember, when taking something, the conscience ripple effect begins, delivering debt toward the future generations in some form.

You shall not bear false witness against your neighbor.
Honesty is still the best policy. Never lie to yourself and others. Unless it is favorable toward transformation, but never be fake.

You shall not covet.
We learned about this one in limited beliefs, "Keeping up with the jones."

I wanted to add this; yes, maybe it turned off a lot of you, but I could have taken these rules and rewritten them in any way I liked and made it into a self-development book. I want to open your mind that the mind's teachings are not new and have traveled since the beginning of time. Somehow, we forgot how powerful we are.

If we look at the past, we will find Maat's rules, the Goddess of truth, justice, wisdom, the stars, law, morality, order, harmony, the seasons, and cosmic balance. All I am saying is to feed your mind and grow into your definitions.

Exercise:
Read up on the Ten Commandments and Maat if you want. Write something about how each one can help someone in life regarding desires, law of attraction, spirituality, or anything you are looking for in life. And come back to this in time and see if you grew into new definitions. The Ten Commandments are the living law. No, that does not say it changes, or we outgrow it, but it lives and grows within all of us—the ingredients of pure energy. We can even turn all of these into the positive. What are the commandments positively, and how can we utilize the rule to direct our minds toward financial and life growth?

I hope this book's design can help teach you how to develop your conscience, subconscious, thought, and emotional patterns—not in the wrong way, only in the right ways to do the exercises in this book. I am not trying to make you believe in something other than yourself. I could have quickly taken this part out of the book. I only want to show you some are tricked into living out the laws or spend a lifetime denying them. You can take these tools above and rewrite them any way you see fit as a guide for yourself.

#1 _____
_____
_____
_____

#2 _____
_____
_____

#3 _____
_____
_____

#4 _____
_____
_____

#5 _____
_____
_____

#6 _____
_____
_____

#7 _____
_____
_____

#8 _____
_____
_____

#9 _____
_____
_____

#10 _____
_____
_____

I found that if we deny the great Architect rule or whatever label we choose, we deny ourselves. Do unto your neighbor as you would want done to you. Again, we look outside of us, yes how we treat others is what reflects and returns to us, but we tend to deny our meaningful purpose and that great neighbor is also ourselves. it was me not accepting and ignoring the Guide of Divine. The law of accepting. Did your mind leave the above exercise alone because of a belief, or did a label turn you off? If so, stop and think for a moment.

The Guide needs to become us, for we are the workers of now and the future. What we deny or what we accept become the next generations unless we are trained in the art of directing our lives with a positive outlook.

Want to blow your mind open? Consider everything to be the Guide to directing the mind. All men and women are created equal but will live out their lives at the level of the mind's eye it believes. Most of those projections in the eyes of the mind are other people's ideas.

One can only guide those with reflection, and the only way to advance your review is to increase what you believe. Believing in a Higher Power is remarkable toward courage, faith, and strength. I warn you that putting all your energy being obsessed with a Higher Power is not healthy if you do not think for yourself and strengthen yourself. Some use The Name as an excuse.

One cannot believe in something more significant if they do not have faith in themselves.

The self is the missing ingredient. Believing in a Higher Power or secret, mystery, or magic without acting on self can cause a downward spiral or a stale an idle life. Some may become frustrated and annoyed as an excuse; they have never positively pursued a meaningful purpose. Or some may direct their entire life consuming material objects or finding happiness in fear or anger or illnesses. Love, healthy pride, and a positive outlook are missing in such people's lives.

Those who do not believe in themselves become angry at the world and at successful people. These people buy excuses from the money rich and eventually accept others' excuses as their own and begin to create that idea into the mind. That mind creation will reflect outward and direct one's life and may even control the future to come.

At this time, it is impossible to understand the mind with words, definitions, or labels. Many have tried. Only to confuse and blind many and prevent them from believing in themselves and their real intentions and dreams. This is exactly why the secrets to the mind stay hidden in plain sight.

If we learn how to silence the outside noise and learn to listen to the silence, the Guide to the mind will reveal itself. This information cannot be burned or destroyed. It is the law of the Universe.

I do have some potent mind tools that I have used to teach myself about what I call listening to silence, or, as I also call it, "Annoy the heck out of the negative." The teaching alone is a book by itself. These teachings will be part of my workbook series or one-on-one coaching. It is coming soon.

The problem is not that the media is hostile and filled with harmful noise; it is that. The press caters to the masses. Yes, maybe you can become more money successful by selling to the negative, but look at the faces of the people who sell this. Yes, it may be what the masses believe they want, but someone in the sale of negative is the same as taking without giving or receiving what you serve. We now understand not to sell the negative, for it goes against our success morals and will deteriorate our minds in some form. We should pass success to others because sensation returns to us in many ways, not just in the pocket. That is the hidden truth of riches.

13

Master Mind

*If you find yourself weak in persistence, surround yourself with a **master mind** group.*

— **Napoleon Hill**

It seems like every place we look; someone is building a master mind group. But like the multiple definitions of success, there are many different levels and descriptions of the master mind alliance.

The automaker Henry Ford's master mind story appears in Napoleon Hill's writings. A newspaper attacked Henry Ford in the headlines, calling Henry Ford an ignorant man. Ford decided that he was going to sue the newspaper company. In court, the newspaper tried to use political and historical questions to prove that Ford was ignorant. People knew Ford as being street-smart, not school-smart.

Ford proved that even if he built himself from poverty, he had formed a group of people with all kinds of knowledge. He told the court that he may not know everything about history—Ford called it useless information, and he had more critical things to do with his time—but on his desk was a button that, at any time, could reach someone to answer any question needed on any subject at any time—proving that he was not an ignorant man.

Ford built a master mind alliance; His street-smart and successful mindset attracted some of America's richest men of his time. He filled in for what the very wealthy non-street-smart people didn't have, a connection between the minds of the richest men in the world.

It is not knowledge that attracts your master mind alliance; it is your level of attitude. The reflection of your mindset is the level of your mental attitude. Why do you think that the most powerful men in America in Ford's time wanted to master mind with Ford? Because Ford's personality helped empower them. Make no mistake—knowledge is worthless if you never take action. We can pretty much say that action attracts action. Successful people want to be inspired by their surroundings. It is not that successful people dislike the negative or the idle mindset/outlook It is that the real successful people wish to spend their time inspired in a positive direction. Do not get me wrong; you can also have a master mind alliance for the negative and idle.

During my mental self-healing journey, I developed myself out of the old me and my old surroundings. I left behind the old levels and the people that I believed were successful and those that I looked up to. The law of growth will push everything you do not need in your life and will direct you toward everything you need in your life. The hardest part that you will face is the argument you have within and not allowing your security blankets to fade away quickly. Some security blankets can be relationships, family members, locations, life friends, and beliefs. Remember, it is you who is accepting the new world which will end up repelling the old.

It is not that the old world is awful, or that you do not like the old world. It is just that the people living in the old world want to stay behind. It is not up to you to change anyone but yourself. The pathway less traveled is going to be hard enough to travel alone. Do not add weight to your journey; if they are supposed to be part of your journey, they will lead with you or catch up to you one day.

How do we take action to build a real master mind alliance?

Napoleon Hill wrote the book *Think and Grow Rich*. The secret to success is in the title. But everyone's mindset chooses to read what they choose to read. Many (including me) read the "think" and "rich" part. I searched for an easy way to money and ignored the word "Grow" in the title. The secret to any level of your success is the level of your mind, beliefs, and energy. If you grow all of these, you boost your master mind alliance. Remember, character attracts character, like attracts like, mental attitude attracts the same mental attitude. Do you understand why success will most likely become a lonely road until you leave the old self behind?

I have witnessed many people trying to attract and build a master mind alliance to cover up their fears and bad habits. One must grow in mind and reality.

It is said you become the five books you read and the five people you surround yourself with. It is easy to read five books, but how do you build a master mind alliance without knowing anyone successful? Yes, you can network. You can join local master mind groups, whatever they are.

Networking takes a lot of work. Maybe you are shy, traumatized in some form. Perhaps you are uncomfortable around new people. Fear is real. I offered to help others network. I even said I would speak for them, rent a table with them, and so on. But because of the fear they created excuses for themselves. How much more can a guide do for someone else? Therefore, I believe most coaching system designs are to sell to the negative. And most master mind alliance groups do not know what it takes to create a master mind alliance.

How do we start when we are alone on our journey, and all we know are people we do not want to become? How do we build a team?

We need to become great partners with our other-selves. We need to have the most extraordinary master mind alliance with ourselves. Boom, let that sink in. Again. The habit of looking outside of us gives us an excuse that we do not hold the hidden truths inside us.

When I started my business, I held a lot of fear and arguments in my mind. I still had not understood success. Unconsciously I looked for people to take over my fears—my first attempt at building a master mind alliance. I realized I was attracting the same attitudes as I had into my business, but I did not see it at the time. I let things slide because I did not want to face them. I paid hard in debt and stress.

I even tried opening a business with someone else, and it turned into a toxic relationship with me walking away from thousands upon thousands of dollars. Later, I found the connection. The connection was a connection to the family over twenty-five years ago. In spite of all my preaching about self-development, I still never understood or took control of an essential master mind alliance, and that is the one in my head. This is why I tell you to ignore the law of attraction. The law of attraction is a limited belief and can guide you in the wrong direction in your life if you never fully take control of your mind, and to do so, you have to take action in the mind, in the physical.

Now networking, I found some great people, but it is essential to grow out of your networking groups. It got to the point that most of the group stopped growing. They became stale, only seeking business leads and jobs to build the money count to impress other groups and the top organizers, destroying the group's character. I started to recognize life group members. Elevator speeches became repetitive with no energy, some sitting with no excitement in their words. Maybe they stopped believing in themselves, or they were networking as a form of hanging out. One day I sat at the table and looked around the room, and I found most if not all people had stopped growing or were not happy with the lives they had built. I said to myself, "If I want to grow, I need to leave the group." I could not surround myself with these people anymore.

I trusted a mortgage person to guide me, maybe because of my fears, or perhaps I wanted to be loyal to a networking group. Let us say this put a financial toll on me for about three years. I hired business coaches. One gave me a test, and after the test told me, he had to figure out how to teach me.

I realized my mind was growing out of my surroundings. I probably would not last two days networking with the same groups when I started. Yes, I have a few great contacts and customers, and I am also a customer of people from that group.

When I network, it is never for sales, but to become better self. The key to networking teams is relationships and trust. I have customers from old networking groups tell me that they will use my business no matter what. I also know of people that sat next to me and gave leads to other HVAC contractors, not in the group.

At the beginning of my business, I listened to others telling me I need to get in with contractors and investors. I will say to you today, I only found a couple of people I will deal with, and if I had focused solely on these groups, I would probably have lost my business and mind.

Many success and business coaches have bought into a program; many never overcame any obstacles of life. Everyone wants to be a coach, with most of them never having the courage to face their dreams. I know what it is to step into the unknown, and I am building a learning program with a workbook. Crisis to Riches only scratches the surface of what is to come. When I coach others in my philosophy or Napoleon Hill's principles, I get it all the time sitting with clients on the first day. "Wow, I have been to many coaches. You took me the furthest in one hour."

Before I give any information, I need to have witnessed it for myself, and I need to see it in the other person in some form. I have meetings, and people ask me about the program and get a booklet. I tell them I cannot write a handout for a one-on-one meeting if I do not know anything about them. I need to find out who they are to adjust the learning process. We all learn in different ways. I have a troubleshooting/problem-solving background. It is how my mindset is programmed. I have twenty-four years in the art of troubleshooting HVAC systems. I have learned the mechanical world patterns and the HVAC patterns are the same as a person's patterns. It is Nature in a mechanical form, and we are naturally in the state of a body and mind. There is only one natural law. We live in the patterns or out of Nature's designs. Like an HVAC system, if not maintained right, the system eventually destroys itself faster than Nature would.

Let us not look for a master mind alliance without having control of ourselves, without maintaining our being and maintaining our minds. Chaos and clutter in the mind equal chaos and clutter in the real world and the body. To form a true alliance, we need to reflect on a new level, and the only way to do that is to push into the next level yourself. As Carnegie put it, the master mind alliance is a revolving door. You need to remove everything you do not need to make room for success. It will happen in layers.

We hear the unhappy money- and material-rich stories, but we never hear how they got themselves there. They had built their minds in one direction without finding full balance. They gave up something for their financial wealth.

First, to attract a powerful master mind alliance, we need to grow into it; second, we need to become it first to attract it unless you have the funds to hire them. It is essential to become financially abundant in the money world, but we can overspend our lives in the process.

Energy is needed to balance our lives. When I eat wrong and do not work out, I become drained and lose my power in which I give up time. Time is valuable, and it is all that we have. We have all been giving time abundantly, and the only difference between the successful and non-successful people is how one uses their time; time is spent according to the mindset of the people. Want to change anything? Change the perspective of the people that will transform attitude, and attitudes will build and heal reality.

My mother's death was from childhood diabetes. In my forties, I found that my past downward spiral had caught up with me. I became a diabetic also. Or, my family's imprints of worries were finally created within me. I have not been strong enough to reverse it yet. But maybe that is not my duty on Earth; perhaps my job is to make the next generations stronger through passing positive emotions, beliefs, and strengths into the next generations. Now, I have turned an ailment/crisis into a blessing. If I can help one parent that saves one child, it is all worth it.

I am doing everything in my power to reverse this ailment. It is taking a lot of action to keep my energy up and sugars balanced. OK, maybe you have more control of your body than I currently have. It is hard enough to push through failures, mistakes, financial debt, depression, and stress and add a drained body or mind. It only slows one down from success.

If I eat wrong or do not exercise, I crash hard, and it is

hard to push through that. I need an alliance with my mind and body, and belief system.

We can live over abundantly in one part of our lives as we drain the rest of our life. We can manifest objects, but what are we giving up? Yes, material objects can drive us and be blessings, but if we must sell our balance, is it worth it? For many years I lived life abundantly with fear, anger, alcohol, overeating, being stressed, and hating life, and I had a bank account and had my dad's definition of life. Sometimes we chase things, and we never witness our lives fading or being taken away from us.

I have witnessed people repeatedly say that they need a master mind alliance outside of them to succeed. If you want to achieve significantly, you will need others to do the work for you or guide you. Remember, it takes money to hire or the right mindset to attract who you need or the finances required.

I ask you, do you have a master mind alliance with your mind, or is your mind arguing with itself? Is your mind full of noise? The tools to balance yourself and your financial wealth are out there. When I first started, I hired the wrong people because my mind was not ready. I let economic issues drain my body with worry and stress, taught to me from past generations. Probably dated back to the United States Depression or from the countries my ancestors came. I am the one that chose to wake up and to rewrite my history that is redirecting my future/success.

It is not that I did not have to go through my mistakes and heartaches to become the person I am today. I just wish somehow, in the beginning, I did not feel alone. It was a journey I had to do alone, and to this day, I find myself growing out of my thought patterns and surroundings constantly.

In one dream, I had a message: Why do I beg for advice from those who know less than I do? We go through layers of not trusting ourselves, and we look to less-qualified people for answers. Learn to control your inner worlds, and let the master mind alliance come to you. When you are ready, they will show up. You may even find that they have been in front of you for a long time. Remember, the law of accepting is that the mind can only expect what it accepts.

> *For where two or three are gathered together in my name, there am I in the midst of them.*
> —Matthew 18:20

When the internal mind flows uniformly, the outside noise and the inner argument fade away, and there is something in the middle connecting the senses to a source. This silence is powerful. It took me years to develop pure silence. My workbook will get very deep into this and all of the writings in this book. It will be coming soon.

If you can find any group that drives you, gives you energy, or excites you into action, that is a master mind—food for the thinking.

The best example of a master mind alliance to date is the American Founding Fathers. Look at what a group of minds and applying faith could remove and create and keep in motion for hundreds of years. They understood the so-called secret tools to success and used those tools in mind and reality. Once you tap into Nature's laws, they push you like the wind pushing the sailboat. But trying to sail this boat without guidance following the natural rules would sink the boat.

14

Vision

Vision it, let your mind go to work, allow your mind to lead you, get out of the mind's way, and, most important, it is up to you to get yourself there.

It was one lonely night at the beginning of my journey, searching for enlightenment in self-development, and I came across a picture on the Internet. This picture was a picture of the Napoleon Hill street marker in Virginia.

For those who do not know who Napoleon Hill is, Napoleon Hill is the author of some outstanding success works ever written like, *Think and Grow Rich*, *Law of Success*, *Outwitting the Devil*, *The Golden Rule*, and *Science of Success*. You can find all the information you need about Napoleon Hill at Naphill.org, The Napoleon Hill Foundation.

Staring at the Napoleon Hill street marker's picture on my computer, I closed my eyes and demanded that I take a picture in front of the sign to show the image off to my friends on social media.

With a vivid image in mind, I visioned myself standing

in the grass, taking the picture. I could feel the grass; I could hear the cars driving by, which I know now to be my mind's eye. My vision and the emotion that I fed the image stayed powerful for around three minutes until I opened my eyes.

I had friends in Virginia, and I thought I would visit them and take the picture in front of the sign. I later found out that the state of Virginia is a lot bigger than I believed. The marker and my friends lived over six hours apart. That vision, that foolish vision of showing off, faded away, and I never thought of that marker again.

My success journey was building very slowly. I continued studying and listening to everything about the business, self-development, and spirituality that I could find. I was growing in my business and overcoming my fears and everything that was holding me down. I had also buried myself with a lot of business financial debt. I had made tons of mistakes. It cost money to get my contractor's licenses and took time to study for the tests. I also used self-development as an excuse not to work on my business. My business, and my mindset, went from "paycheck to paycheck" and developed into "work only as hard as I needed to survive." I paid dearly for my fears, worries, limiting beliefs, traumas, procrastination, and chasing a secret to success. The only one I was making rich was my credit card companies. Imagine the toll for me to have this debt weight—thousands of dollars a month for interest alone.

Failing was not an option. I was going to push through everything and everyone that got in my way. People ask me if I would ever go back to work. I say, "I would rather die." See, for me, there is no option but to figure success out. The old me had already died mentally and almost physically as well. The new me was the first time I was alive.

One needs to want success more than they want money. I am telling you, I do not believe focusing only on money is strong enough to overcome the beating most will take in the real world. Almost every town, county, or village wants something, and many decide to create their separate contractors' licensing fees and tests. One county alone had three different licenses with three written examinations and two physical tests.

Money was my first purpose, but the purpose of cash had not driven me. If money were my king, I would have given up a long time ago; money was not worth it. I worked for years for free. I worked for free on development. I worked for free to overcome my fears. I pushed myself and worked paying the endless high-interest debt for years, making the credit card companies rich with business debt. Now add in, most of my work is in the summer working in attics all day. When everyone wants to go out, I am working as many hours as possible I can put in.

I spent a lot of time focusing on myself, and I had the feeling I needed to write about my journey. I felt like many self-development speakers, coaches, teachers, and books had copied other people's ideas in their writings and misguided me on my journey, and that was when the book Self-Heal and Become Success was born. I call it the journey of reading self-development books, the beginning of my spiritual awakening and meeting my messengers/teachers.

Writing the *Self-Heal and Become Success* book cost me more than what I have made from it so far. I did not care or do not care, because I know the information needed to be out there. I was no writer. I did not know anything about publishing. I decided to write to a publishing company for any advice about the manuscript and publishing a book from a book I was studying. I asked if they had any advice for me. I told them, "I have a book about the secret to success that is not a secret at all." I received a letter that stated we do not publish books on that subject or something like that. Maybe they receive emails like that all the time, but it turned me off, and I found it insulting from a self-development publishing company.

I didn't know what to do. I was lost and felt like I was being punched in the gut. One day I visited a local lodge near me. I was looking at the air-conditioning, and they had a flyer of an author visiting and told me it would be fascinating. I said, "Great." The only thing I had in mind was to find out about publishing. Something was telling me that I need to release my writing into the world. At the end of his book review, I asked the author about publishing. The author told me I might want to look into self-publishing. I never knew self-publishing existed.

The journey of self-publishing had begun. I found Amazon had a platform for self-publishing writers. I finally found the strength to proofread the book and published it on Amazon and the Kindle. I was happy I was done and never had to write again. So, I thought.

Writing, reading, and studying were not my desires. It took me four years to pass tenth-grade English. Now I am building an effective technique. These roads of development were not easy for me. Something was driving me because I did not have a purpose or a vision of what I wanted or needed in life.

I was now an author, which helped me a lot with networking and meeting more like-minded people.

The search for the next level had begun. Something was missing, and I needed to find it. I was still struggling, alone, and lost.

I decided to search for what was missing again on the computer. I came across the Napoleon Hill Foundation, and I found that they had a certificate program. My mind told me I needed to get certified. I had no desire to teach, write, or coach anyone; my focus was on the air-conditioning company, but I wanted to know more. I had to find what I was missing and drawn back to Napoleon Hill's work.

The next day I called the foundation, and Don Green answered the phone. We talked about Napoleon Hill and the books *Think and Grow Rich* and *Outwitting the Devil*. He listened to me about my journey and my book. He reassured me that action was vital and that many fail to recognize this. Don Green told me that Napoleon Hill wrote the word "action" seventy-three times in the book *Think and Grow Rich*.

It was the first time on my journey I was talking to someone mind to mind. Don was passionate while he spoke, not only about Napoleon Hill but for me. This phone call changed my life instantly. See, I felt alone on my journey; I had no one to talk to about success. It was the first time I had opened my mind outside of my book. Even when it came to my book, I had not told anyone about it because I feared I would be talked out of it. I also was not sure if I was going crazy or not. See, I held back in my first book because of that fear and the fear of criticism.

That night after the phone call, I signed up for the Napoleon Hill Foundation's PMA (positive mental attitude) Science of Success certification course. The journey of reading and reading had begun. Remember, this was the weakest point of my life, reading and studying, but I had pushed through contractor's license tests before.

The only thing I said to myself was, "No matter what, I would complete this"—that crazy inner drive.

I passed the first levels of the certificate program, and next was to take the final training in person in Wise, Virginia, at the Napoleon Hill Foundation. Again, it was way out of my comfort zone; I was crippled with fears and worried about shutting down my air-conditioning business during the start-up season—my money-making season. The hidden drive overpowered all that was holding me back.

Finally, I went to the foundation and found a classroom full of like-minded people. For the first time in my journey toward success in a new world, I was not alone.

One evening after class, we visited the Napoleon Hill marker, and I was so excited to take a picture. That moment standing there taking that picture, I had that déjà vu feeling that I have been there before. Not until I got back in the car did, I remember that one night's foolish vision.

After completing the next part of the PMA certificate, we, the Napoleon Hill students, received our final exam to complete at home. Part of my exam was to do something using the Science of Success Principle of Self-Discipline. A few months ago, I had finally broken my crippling fear of speaking in front of a room of strangers. I decided to talk about the principle in front of an audience. I studied and studied the principle of self-discipline. I wrote out a speech, and I tried my hardest to remember it word for word.

I could never remember the entire speech; however, trying to do so must have imprinted this principle into my sub-conscious mind. I realized that all this time, what I was missing was self-discipline, and as Napoleon Hill states in his philosophy, "If you have self-discipline, you do not need any other principles."

The Napoleon Hill Foundation gave me what I was seeking as a final, not planned but a random picking. Life/mind/God/Universe will guide you in mysterious ways if you open your mind to it and take action toward growing with it—the journey of overcoming all of your obstacles growing into a higher you. The higher you knows how to direct you toward your meaningful purpose.

I passed my final exam, receiving my PMA Science of Success certificate on April 7, 2019.

June was right around the corner, and the next class was going to meet in Wise, Virginia. As always, a feeling came across me. I was still alone on my journey, and I needed a boost. I reached out to the foundation and asked if I could come. I even said I would hide in the corner. I received an email back, asking me if I was willing to do my final about self-discipline in front of the class. At first, I was confused, for I still argued with my confidence within. I still did not believe I was good enough. I also did not want to be a burden. After I spoke in front of the class, I was blown away by the reaction I received.

My greatest fear had transformed into one of my greatest assets. Not only did my foolish vision get me to the marker, but that simple vision also pushed me to the street marker two years in a row.

My vision was growing beyond anything I had ever imagined. That speech at the foundation led me to a new opportunity to speak for Think and Grow Rich Sweden in Sweden. Now there was fear again. I had never traveled alone; heck, I am from Long Island, and I never took the train into the city by myself. If you fear it, you must face it. Done, I will not get in the way, and I said yes, I would do it. I had to take two planes to get to Stockholm, Sweden. My simple vision guided me to an opportunity to become an international speaker and instructor. From this trip, the other certified instructors and I created the Global Team.

Later on, I was asked to speak for Think and Grow Rich Caribbean and Jamaica Cruise. After the cruise, I decided to set up a PMA Science of Success a day for charity on Long Island, New York. The Global Team—seven of us—had plans to come and speak together. That never happened due to the coronavirus and the New York shutdown of 2020. The New York PMA event was scheduled for Saturday, the day before the New York shutdown. The vision is still growing, and when this coronavirus is gone, we are rocking this world.

Vision it, let your mind go to work, allow your mind to lead you, get out of the mind's way, and, most important, it is up to you to get yourself there.

1. Vision it, demand the mind.
2. Let your mind go to work.
3. Allow your mind to lead you.
4. Most important, it is up to you to get yourself there.

Take your vision in detail, see it in the mind's eye, and feel it with emotions and all of your senses. Become that vision in mind, demand it, and imprint it in mind. Let your mind go to work. Let it work; let it move in a direction that will better yourself. Allow your mind to lead you, have trust in your journey, and always see everything as guidance— everything. Finally, most importantly, get out of your mind's way, and no one will get you there but you. The longer you fight or dwell in your comfort zone, security, the old you, and your-soon-to-be-old surroundings, the longer you will hold down your success. As long as you always grow and push through with a positive mental attitude, the mind will get you there if you let it.

15

Self-Discipline

Inspired by Napoleon Hill's PMA Science of Success Principle, Self-Discipline

Self-discipline. What does self-discipline mean to you? We all know someone who has lost control of their lives and habits due to a lack of self-discipline.

To the best of my belief, self-discipline is one of the most critical and most important success principles that most people fear and put off working on and developing on.

Why do I believe this?

When you start working on the success principle of self-discipline, it will force you to break away from your comfort zone. You will find your surroundings changing; you must confront the inner you, and you better be ready to take on the inner self. You will find yourself encountering and eliminating everything that you fear, and your world will shift inside and out.

Facing oneself is terrifying for many to confront and conquer, causing many to give up on their life journey of living out their desires.

The most strenuous conflict you are ever going to face

is within yourself. If you lack self-discipline, you will never, ever be able to overcome the person within that is holding you down from building your Definite Major Purpose into reality. The experience you have been born to live out will fade away.

Every day, every night, you need to overcome everything that holds you down, no matter how long it takes or how many habits and thought patterns you need to transform in the direction toward the pathway of living life with a blissful state of mind.

Recover and develop your purpose with the tool of self-discipline.

No other single requirement for individual success is as important as self-discipline. Self-discipline or self-control means to take possession of your own mind. (Napoleon Hill)

What is self-discipline:

- To take possession of your own mind
- The only thing over which you have complete, unchallenged control is your power of thought
- Developing control over yourself, developing control over your mind, focusing on the things you want, and ignoring the things you do not want is essential to achieving success.
- Self-discipline starts with the mastery of your own thoughts. If you do not control your thoughts, you cannot control your deeds.

Benefits which mastery of self-discipline will bring you:

- Your imagination will become more alert.
- Your enthusiasm will become keener.
- Your initiative will become more active.
- Your reliance will become greater.
- The scope of your vision will be widened
- Your problems will melt away.
- You will look at the world through different eyes.
- Your personality will become more magnetic.
- Your hope and your ambitions will be stronger.
- Your faith will be more powerful.

What are some simple habits that hold people down from not having the full discipline or full focus on their thoughts, emotions, energy, and lives?

- Appetite for food and drink
- Mental attitude
- Use of time
- Definiteness of purpose

Are your habits controlling you, or are you managing your habits?

Food
What happens when we overeat?

- Feel run down
- Heavy
- Tired

Some people may become depressed, which can drive people to more eating, which eventually causes the body and especially the digestive system to overwork to survive and fight off illnesses. The cells in our body need our help to fight off diseases and stress before the body starts to weaken our thoughts, emotions, and energy, leaving us with less power and drive to live out our passions and may even shorten our life.

You would not run an expensive sports car with the wrong gas, would you? We are priceless, and it is time we start treating ourselves as priceless.

Drink
Some people may say they need a drink or two for social reasons, or maybe they deserve it for working a stressful workday. I needed the bottle. I don't need a bottle or even a drink anymore. I decided one day, I did not want to slow down my growth anymore. I stopped having a drink. I wanted to succeed in life. I now have more productive days than unproductive days. I would love to tell you halting the alcohol was an overnight repair. It was not; it took years of developing my disciplines. This time it has been the longest I have been without a drink, and for the first time, I have no desire ever to drink again. I do not want to slow down my growth, even for a thousandth of a second. I want to live and grow every moment of my life. I always want full control of my mind and my actions.

What if I told you that mental attitude could also be addictive, and your mental attitude can create happiness or destroy happiness? What can we expect from life from transforming a negative mental attitude into a positive mental attitude?

A person with a positive mental attitude finds the following:

- Harmony in human relationships
- Freedom from fear
- Hope from achievement
- Capacity for faith
- An open mind on all subjects
- Sound physical health

When you have self-discipline and you have developed a positive mental attitude, you will find the good in everything. You will see that life is a blessing, and you will find guidance to more significant influences in your life.

A person with a negative mental attitude will not recognize that the mind and attitude attract other minds with the same attitude.

While your thoughts, ideas, and emotions start to develop into a positive mental attitude, you will begin to draw the same.

Your life and relationships will begin to flow into harmony. Your fears will melt away, for you will find you are overcoming all your worries.

You will recognize that completion is hiding behind your most significant fears.

Your hope will rise, and you will witness that you are starting to achieve your goals toward your passions, which will drive you to have faith.

You will find the tools and courage needed to put your faith, your desires into action.

By opening your mind, you will receive guidance, and others will be willing to open their minds to you.

You will start to notice that the level of your thought attracts the same level of thinking. You will begin to build a burning desire for life.

With that burning desire, you will look for sound health. Experience would be exciting for you.

You will want to have full control of all your energy and thoughts to drive you toward the road of abundance.

You will grow into recognizing your definition of success. Everything you do not wish for, or are not, will repel away from you.

Time
We are all wealthy with an abundance of time. How many of us have spent most of our time living out someone else's definition of happiness?

How you spend your time can create a fulfilled life or reverse your life's power and strength.

Many spend their spare time against themselves. How do you spend your extra time?

Before 2014, I was not using my time and especially my spare time toward my dreams. I wasted years and years talking about the end of the world, zombies, and how to survive the "end of time." As if surviving the end of time would be more comfortable than creating my dreams.

Now, almost all of my time is spent to develop my life, attitude, and character, especially my spare time.

Most of my extra time is toward health, business, and networking with and searching for like-minded people.

You are the energy you spend during your free time. Most will overspend their time on the negative.

Invest your time wisely and always, always grow toward a richer you.

Definite purpose

- The starting point in the development of self-discipline is definite purpose.
- Definite purpose is the starting point of all achievement.

Developing control over yourself, improving control over your mind, focusing on the things you want, and ignoring the things you do not wish for is essential to achieving success.

Can you see how important it is to focus on a definite primary purpose with a burning desire? It is essential because it will keep you excited and motivated to create self-discipline of your mind and body.

I have witnessed that many people may be confused about their definite purpose. If you do not recognize a purpose, then make "yourself" your mission by working on your thoughts, actions, and character. Focus on growing a higher you. In all that you do. Everything you do.

It is OK, for it took me years to develop into having a significant purpose in life. Expanding your mind will open the doors toward your real goals; have faith it will, and act at once when those ideas reveal themselves to you.

I want to give you a tool to take home. I have found that many people procrastinate or may not know their purpose. I believe this single tool is essential for one to develop. If you cannot see your life mission yet, start with the smallest step possible; pick anything you want to accomplish, and begin acting on your ideas. You will eventually grow into your meaningful purpose.

- WRITE OUT YOUR DEFINITE MAJOR PURPOSE
- MEMORIZE IT AND REPEAT IT OVER AND OVER
- MAKE IT A RITUAL EVERY DAY AND INTO EVERY NIGHT

Hang it on a wall that you pass every day. Hang it up in the bathroom if you must. You will find that one day your mind will show you the way.

The so-called secret is to learn how to retrain the subconcious through repetition. The subconscious gets into the pattern of believing and creating what it sees visually and hears often.

This above chapter on self-discipline was from my final speech. I want to add something now. I have found many people give up or pass this tool up because they do not have a definite purpose. However, the above three steps are decisive.

Write out your definite purpose. It does not matter what you write, for what is essential is to give your mind a seed/imprint to develop. You and your mind must work together, and you need to have some kind of direction. If you have anything you want to complete in a short time or a lifetime, then make that your purpose. If you want money, make that your purpose.

Suppose you have a small purpose: a new car or an apartment. In the chapter on the power of vision, I showed you one way to imprint with an image. Now we are going to do it with writing. Write out your purpose, no matter how small it is. If it is money, write out how much you want. Write out the time in you wish to receive this purpose and what you are willing to give in return to obtain this purpose. Read it twice a day and make it a ritual.

Again, it is a tool that many skip, and it is a vital tool toward manifesting and accepting. It is the beginning of training the mind to find what you want in life, even if you cannot see it yet. Remember my foolish vision and how far my mind got me so far? Do not forget the fears and obstacles that the inner drive I had pushed me through.

My purpose is
_____
_____
_____

I will receive my purpose at the date of _____

I am willing to provide
_____
_____
_____to obtain my purpose.

16

Institutionalized

Breaking Mental Chains

My father was an NYPD detective and a lieutenant, and some stories he told me shaped my life or saved my life.

One story that stuck in my mind was about this little girl who was kidnapped and institutionalized by her kidnappers.

The story started with my dad telling me how he could not understand that when the police arrested the kidnappers and were inside the kidnapper's house, this little girl ran back into the closet where the kidnappers had held her hostage.

This little girl was finally free, and she ran back to what had become her mental comfort zone. How many little girls are living their adult lives institutionalized in some form of childhood trauma? Maybe not running into a security closet but running mentally into what became a comfort zone, a security blanket.

"What does it mean to be institutionalized? Being **institutionalized means** that a **person** has been locked up long enough that they have become used to it, and this can create problems upon one's release. Prison has a very different culture and day-to-day life than life on the outside, and if you spend long on the inside, you quickly become used to it." - Internet.

In this chapter, I am not talking about physical prisons; however, if we live in a mental prison of the mind, does our mind create that emotion into mental chains that build our reality in some form?

Are there many people living with mental chains from something that their past has created into their reality in some form? Could people be living in a mind mental institute from their past generations? If you never release this or at least witness this, will you pass these emotions and feelings on to the next generations?

I believe self-healing your way toward a blissful state of mind is the secret to your success. How does one do this? They must transform their diversity, failure, and negative life patterns into a blessing, an asset.

Let us build our blessings, not our beliefs.

We all see it. Some people seem to have everything—fame, money, big houses, etc. Yet they lose control of their lives. Why? They never broke out of that closet, their comfort zone, their mental chains. They did everything possible to cover their pain. The mind knows no difference; it reacts to and creates what you give it.

Many will build their hidden emotions and pains into reality in some form. I have.

How do we start to transform diversity, failure, and trauma into a blessing?

- Always outdo the yesterday self in a positive, productive way.
- Shut down the noise.
- Learn to shift negative emotions and thought patterns on the spot.
- Learn to listen to silence; silence is the place you can find self and guidance.
- Find a way to protect yourself from overpowering negative emotions and thoughts.
- Find the blessing in everything.
- Look at the past as a road map to success.

No matter how bad you believe the past is, holding your crisis or trauma inside or trying to hide from it will not helping anyone, especially not you. Chances are someone had it a lot worse than you. By releasing this pain, you may recognize you are not alone in your journey, and others may need your guidance.

We have just started transforming our mental patterns into a blessing, an asset.

When you look at your past as a guide, you can find the blessings in everything if you allow it. Yes, the fight within will hold one down—the security blanket, the secure job, and the safe life.

Why do people deny their journey? They deny facing inward and allowing their quest to release their pain and to release the pain of their ancestors.

For many, suffering has become their comfort zone. We hold on to this suffering as if it is normal; well, for most, it becomes routine; look around, and you will find almost everyone or everyone is comfortable in mental pain, almost as if they enjoy it. As if they have become institutionalized with the reality they have been given.

Yes, maybe some will become richer with money. I will ask, are they also rich in the mind and heart?

What if you have something holding you back, and you do not remember any trauma? What if the mental injury that you have was someone else's in the past? Past generation emotional and thought patterns are passed on to you. I ask this, how many in your family tree have repeated this imprint in some form?

Are you the one that will be the first to step up and stop this trauma or repeated generational patterns and transform it into a blessing?

The work we do on our journey is not easy for many, for this work needs to be from within the self. That scares many people. It scared me to look within myself. Most of my life was all about looking for excuses for why I was not ready.

It is time to recognize the chains that hold us down from our desires, and it is up to us to destroy these restraints. No one will do it for us.

Only until we break everything that is holding us down will we find we are guiding others, and we will recognize that those that we conduct the most will teach us the greatest.

You do get what you give. When you begin receiving in return, your abundance finds you. When you start returning2success, you open yourself to your purpose, your blessings.

You are the law in the law of attraction. Self-heal the law, and transform your attraction. What you accept becomes you—law of accepting. Let us self-heal and accept our journey.

17

The Hidden Truth

Let the mind teach you. The journey, God, Jesus, angels, messengers, mind are all powerful, but belief needs to come from you and from within. It is up to you to take any teaching of your desires and create the life you have been born to live out. God wants you rich. And the journey reveals the understanding of the Guide of Divine.

Remember this: you cannot take without giving something in return. It is the law of Nature. It is the law of conscious living. Law of attraction—everyone tries to attract without giving. Understand this: everyone is giving and receiving at every moment.

Every generation, every moment, we may be aware of something new. Maybe one day you awake and find the world is going in a different direction. Perhaps you witness a downward spiral effect or an upward effect. Remember, for the most part, we must direct our minds only to notice the positive. However, we can never forget the world we left behind, for it seems that it is the world that will eventually catch up, maybe not in our lifetime but down the generation line.

Global limited beliefs are powerful, and so are negative global views. See, not only did I remove layers and layers of harmful patterns, but I also removed layers and layers of limiting beliefs. I am still uncovering and overcoming new layers; at the same time, I am being pulled backward by the world around me.

We come to a point in our lives where we must decide whether to stay in the decay or move toward healing and growth, living abundantly in the positive. Remember, we can also live life abundantly in harmful lifestyles. It is crucial to direct your mind, but it is more important to find balance in your entire life. Balance of mind, energy, money, and family is how you find a blissful state of mind.

At times your journey may feel like a tug of war, pulling you back to the old while you find a hidden drive, the hidden truth pushing you forward. You may not understand what is giving you the strength to overcome obstacles in your life. And no matter how many times you may drift backward, the hidden truth pulls you back up. As if this energy has a mind of its own.

This hidden drive is what reveals your meaningful purpose in life. It teaches and guides you toward the true you, and you start getting a taste of life. Thus, it becomes harder and harder to fall and more and more comfortable to catapult yourself forward.

The hidden truth lies in the journey. One of the most powerful stories that attempt to explain the hidden truth is the journey of Jesus. I am not talking about a building, a story, or outside belief without experience. To understand the secret/hidden truth teachings that I call the hidden drive from within, one must appreciate life's journey and natural laws.

We are no different from anything else in this world. We grow, we stay still, or we decay faster than we are supposed to. The only secrets to any riches are growing into those riches. God wants you rich, and God wants you to respect the means that are accepted by you. To appreciate the hidden truth's abundance, you must push through everything that holds you down from this hidden drive. And sorry, this journey will most likely have to be done alone in the physical world. You will find messengers, teachers, and people looking to take the weight from you. But you cannot take without giving something in return.

The mind or spiritual world is the place you will find control and strength. Remember, to indeed be successful is to control the two worlds that one lives in: the mind/spiritual world and reality/physical world. To receive an abundance of your meaningful purpose, you must take full control of both worlds.

What you are saying right now in your mind are excuses.

The most challenging truth that holds us down is the argument within, the excuses we allowed others and ourselves to feed us. The stories that we allowed to create us. Remember, in the beginning, was the word. Manifesting begins with the word, name, vision, belief, and the direction in which we direct our energy. The only fault we ever faced was not recognizing that something or someone else was in control, and it may even come from those that never understood what they have done. Forgive them for they do not or did not know or understand what they have done or are doing.

They say Jesus will come again. It is the moment that the shift begins. A choice comes in front of us—Barabbas vs. Jesus.

You can witness this battle, maybe in your mind, perhaps in others. You may even notice this fight on the news, social media, and reality at this moment. This argument we face every day, but some people do not witness their actions. A few will find the way to the hidden truth. Remember, Jesus said, "I am the way." But it takes effort to undertake the journey in the right direction to release this great power we all hold. To the best of my belief, Jesus is the way of life's journey, and it takes action to become the way. This decision is repeated in some form over and over in all the texts I have come across.

You do not read self-development books; you develop into understanding the texts.

Action in the right direction is the key to success. What tools you use is entirely up to you. I have warned you that I used self-development books as an excuse that I could not control my reality. I used reading and studying as a security blanket to not face my hidden truth.

I was scared to face my reality and found myself dwelling in the mind or the spiritual world as an excuse that I was not ready to face myself. I wanted to coach others in success when I was scared to walk my journey.

I watch teachers and writers today repeat the works of others. I watch coaches read texts. I watch healers try to heal others as an excuse not to heal themselves. I watch people every day walk from their hidden drive and dwell in unhealthy lifestyles, hate, etc. I know for I came from every one of those places. Maybe it is the cycle of the journey, and the only key to the hidden drive is to keep moving forward.

Yes, in a money world, we need money to live our dreams, but we cannot let our dreams decay our lives, families, and world. The balance is more important than everything else. The Guide of the Divine. The free will of the people. The freedom of the minds to lead us. If all we are is mind, and we are all one, God connects us all and guides us in ways we can never explain. It is not God that turns on us; it is we that have forsaken ourselves. Face your journey and reveal your hidden truth. The drive will build, and soon the law of momentum will take over, and the spiral upward will begin to run on autopilot, and the attraction will come to you with ease.

Do you recognize why believing in a secret to success, manifesting, law of attraction, and many other definitions are excuses and limiting beliefs? Even the hidden truth is a limited belief. It is only a label that I used to get your attention. In other words, I tricked you in hopes that you understand that you are the hidden truth.

I found a hidden drive within me that gave me the strength to destroy all my obstacles. This drive has pushed me this far, and does not want to stop. It is almost like it keeps picking me up and moving me into the fight. I tell you, this fight fades away.

The key to life's riches is the hidden truth, which is to face what we most fear. The hidden truth is you, the mind; you can recognize what you let go and let in. One must give before they get. Let go of all that you do not need and allow in the life of riches. This is why hate and love cannot exist simultaneously in our minds. It is not that we do not witness the downward spiral; we deny it and deny the hidden truth.

18

Final Chapter

If you only read the first and final chapters, you are not ready yet. Place the book on the shelf, and if or when you are prepared, the book will call you again. Success is not about the first chapter or the final chapter. If you put this book back on the shelf, I fully understand. The book that changed my life sat in my closet for half of my life over twenty years before I prepared myself, and I had to hit rock bottom first.

The road for me was challenging, for I had to unlearn everything I believed and unlearn others' lessons. I had to stop and take control of the downward spiral, called the out-of-control spin to rock bottom, and teach myself how to start to build and climb my way into an upward spiral locating, understanding the hidden truth to riches. If I could make it this far so, can you.

Picking up and completing this book tells me that you are ready to face the hidden truth and work on overcoming all that may hold you down. We have touched on many tools of the hidden secrets to success. Remember this, I am still growing, and the things that I believed in the past were not real. I have uncovered many layers and am still uncovering more today and will most likely continue for the rest of my life. What worked for me may not work for you. I have tried to reveal many definitions of personal tools toward a blissful state of mind.

With this book's tools and text, I hope I have revealed a pathway that allows you to open your mind and take possession of your thoughts, emotions, and reactions. You would have learned how to vision all parts of your life, including your future, and how to create your definitions as you level up. The level of your description is the level of the mind, the status of your success.

I started this journey alone. I did not know of any groups like the Napoleon Hill Foundation training, Meetups, Toastmasters, real-estate investors, and social networks. I did not realize self-development books because I hated to read. All I knew was the thoughts someone or something else had mastered my entire life and trained me to let others do my thinking.

We can now teach ourselves how to think for ourselves.

Remember that you may need to find a way to protect yourself as your mind opens and starts to clear out. The breakthroughs may not be yours, but someone else's in the past. Emotions imprinted in the blueprints are delivered to you. When my affirmation was not strong enough, I used prayer (Our Father). My spiritual/energy guru told me that I should memorize the prayer before knowing that I needed its strength. One can use mantras also. Remember that prayers are powerful affirmations. My workbook and one-on-one will get deeper into the power of affirmations. Keep a lookout for my future work.

The crisis of 2020 has resulted in the loss of many dreams and businesses. Sadly, I believe everyone's ideas are essential. I think feeling good about yourself and building a company or confidence can help provide happiness all around. I am now watching storefronts on Long Island opening for rent all over the place. Dreams crushed. Financial bailouts can only get you so far if you do not shift your focus patterns.

The news programs decided not to show people how to shift their thinking or think out of the box in these challenging times. Buy a Negative Mental Attitude or buy a Positive Mental Attitude. The choice is yours. I understand that the business selling the negative is profitable. Most choose to buy adversely. One cannot fail if they can shift their vision, thoughts, ideas, and words. They are the ones that can turn any crisis into riches, whether they find the hidden truth or not. The one thing they find is the power of direction.

Leaders are born already, maybe not woken yet; the seed has not rattled loose. You are the leader, and I hope this book rattled your leadership's origin, the hidden skills needed in this vast world.

I want to thank all my readers who took time out of their lives to finish this book and share the text with others. I am proud of you and all that you have done till this moment, and I am proud of what you will do with this information for yourself and others.

IN GOD, WE MUST TRUST

Made in the USA
Middletown, DE
19 June 2024